Ensimismamiento

LANE CARNES

Copyright © 2024 Lane Carnes.

All rights reserved. No part of this book may be reproduced, stored, or transmitted by any means—whether auditory, graphic, mechanical, or electronic—without written permission of both publisher and author, except in the case of brief excerpts used in critical articles and reviews. Unauthorized reproduction of any part of this work is illegal and is punishable by law.

This is a work of fiction. All of the characters, names, incidents, organizations, and dialogue in this novel are either the products of the author's imagination or are used fictitiously.

ISBN: 978-1-63950-219-6 (sc)
ISBN: 978-1-63950-220-2 (e)

This publication contains the opinions and ideas of its author. It is intended to provide helpful and informative material on the subjects addressed in the publication. The author and publisher specifically disclaim all responsibility for any liability, loss, or risk, personal or otherwise, which is incurred as a consequence, directly or indirectly, of the use and application of any of the contents of this book.

Writers Apex

Gateway Towards Success

8063 MADISON AVE #1252
Indianapolis, IN 46227
+13176596889
www.writersapex.com

www.cacbethel.com
www.igoeministry.com

CONTENTS

Chapter 1 Nickel Plated Belt Buckle 1

Chapter 2 Basketball and Existentialism 42

Chapter 3 Ruminations in Missouri and New York 69

Chapter 4 Thoughtful Reflections 91

Chapter 5 Kansas City and the Classics 112

Chapter 6 Musings on Adolescence 131

Chapter 7 Final Introspections 149

Dedication and in Memory of Mrs. Joan Bruder

This book is dedicated to many people who have influenced and loved me from the time I was an infant, born in Independence, Missouri, but raised in San Juan, Puerto Rico. First, I am grateful for all of God's blessings beginning with thanking my parents, Nat and Connie, two of the most unselfish, loving, and caring people a son could ever imagine having for their steadfast love and encouragement. Secondly, I am also privileged to have a beautiful sister, Rene, with whom I shared many of the experiences delineated in this *novella* and who I love dearly.

In addition, I would like to thank Jan, my precious wife and life's companion, for encouraging, supporting, and allowing me the space for this creative endeavor. The completion of this work is a testament to our relationship founded on the principle underscored in Corinthians:

"Love is the greatest and strongest of all emotions that keeps two people together."

Finally, I would like to dedicate this book honoring the life of Joan, my "saintly" mother-in-law, and her endearing family from New Orleans, Louisiana. Joan was a woman with a magnetic smile and a love for every person she encountered. Her smile remains with all of us today. I will always remember Joan raising both arms in response to the victorious athletes of the 2012 Olympics, a moment Jan and I shared with her as we watched the games from her television set in Picayune, Mississippi. This endearing image of her rests in my heart and is solidified by Jan's deep love for her expressed in the tenderness of their numerous hugs.

NICKEL PLATED BELT BUCKLE

Lance woke up early in the morning with a discomforting and protracted lump in his throat. He felt like he shouldn't discuss what was about to ensue in the schoolyard today with his family. In a way, he wished he would have fought Anselmo yesterday, so he wouldn't have to think about it any longer. Lance was disrespected in school in front of others; this was the ultimate blow to his person, God, and his complete identity as a Latin. Although Lance was not a native Hispanic, he quickly adapted to the Puerto Rican culture, especially after growing up on the island and attending Spanish public schools from the third through the ninth grades. Lance knew now, as an older man, that this fight was representative of the rift that existed between the United States and a Hispanic country like Puerto Rico divided by borders of different languages and cultural values.

He, as a North American adolescent, had the unique opportunity of *infiltrating* this divide with his fist at first. Later, he developed a profound appreciation for the great connection between the two countries joined politically as a Commonwealth (Estado Libre Asociado) in 1952. Puerto Rico retained Spanish as its official language despite the urgency many islanders espoused in becoming a state of the U.S. with English becoming the predominant language. The North Americans evolved into a great country composed of immigrants who assimilated to the American lifestyle underscored by the English language as the common denominator. Adversely, though, the United States had difficulty retaining its credibility globally in the 21st century, since it has carved out an isolationist stance when attempting to understand the complexities of Latin America, the Middle East, Africa, and other parts of the world. This occurred unintentionally, since America was a superpower for many decades, which culturally required others to learn English to participate in the global economic community. Conversely, few in the United States anticipated the shift in economics due the Chinese boom and the instability caused by the Islamic State in the Syrian Civil War that would prompt Americans to be more interested in other cultures. This delay in understanding others is also due to the technological advancement of the United States juxtaposed greatly by its unconscious neglect to acculturate its people. Realizing that respect, humility, and goodwill towards others are accomplished only through learning each other's language fluently. Then, one can truly say: "He is my brother because he has painstakingly taken the time to learn my language, and conversely, I learned his."

Delighting in his *fluir de la conciencia (*flow of consciousness*)* musings, Lance opined that bad thoughts are definitely more stressful than the actual punches he might give or receive. He tried to think positively by repeating the following syllogism to himself: "¡Los chicos valientes son victoriosos!" (Brave boys are victorious!) Lance returned to *reality* as he dressed himself and made sure he wore his favorite belt with the large nickel buckle. He inspected the metallic *weapon* carefully to make sure it was securely fastened and hoped this would be his lucky day; his reticence went unnoticed at the breakfast table.

The rays of golden sunlight reflected off the blue green ocean as the waves crashed on the sand of the impeccably idyllic Caribbean beach in San Juan, Puerto Rico. Men, as far back as 624 B.C., specifically, Thales of Miletus, the first Western Greek philosopher of our culture, who believed everything came into being by water, have always admired the ocean and its magical cyclical movements. He coined the phrase: "The earth floats on the water like a log." The sublime beauty and mystery of the sea continued to mystify and befuddle John Sullivan, Lance's father. John preferred to speak in Spanish after leaving Mercedes, Texas where he was confounded by the extreme prejudice there against Hispanic students who were disciplined by etching on the board over and over again: "I will not speak Spanish." "No hablaré español".

Today, as a teacher at Poteet ISD in South Texas, Lance was asked by a naive, young, Chicana, wannabe gangster: "Do you know what a *tear drop* is Mr. Sullivan?" "Sí, mija… it means I shot someone in the back… I'm a real **COBARDE (COWARD)**, ésa…"

She rolled her eyes and said: "Fuck you!" This is the usual lingo of the few wannabes who think they are *chévere* (cool)!! A common vernacular phrase used by many young adolescents influenced by pop culture and ignored by the present superintendent, Mr. Valenzuela, who is more concerned about his legacy than the true education of primarily poor and unprivileged Hispanic children. He is a leader with a "cara de nopal." In Mexico, this means he is Hispanic because his face metaphorically looks like the predominant nopal cactus. This idiomatic image associates his appearance as being a Latin but without the ability to speak Spanish. Unfortunately, many Hispanics in Texas and the Southwestern states deny their heritage because they don't speak Spanish and have no desire to do so. It is shameful that a leader does not take the initiative to be true to oneself and to the children he is privileged to educate by learning the language of their ancestors.

The azure sky with white embedded clouds overlooked the small island, approximately hundred miles long and forty wide. The Black-African slaves settled in Puerto Rico and various Caribbean islands after the Spaniards and other Europeans enslaved and brought them from Africa to the *New World* in the 15th and 16th centuries and later. The slaves were forced to work mining for gold and silver, and they also labored on the sugar plantations. The African, the indigenous *Taíno*, and Spanish cultures are the three predominant ethnic groups of Puerto Rican society responsible for blending their languages, art, music, and other aspects of their rich heritages, creating an incredibly beautiful syncretistic ethnicity.

Older now, a more mature Lance would lose himself poetically by extrapolating and synthesizing this image of *Borinquén* (Land of the Valiant Lord—the pre-Spaniard name designated to the island by its native people, the Taínos) in a *free wheeling* moment of French creativity: "*Cette île magnifique où les reflets du soleil encore donne aux eaux les images des vagues de la mer qui persistent dans la voix de Thales qui résonne chaque matin et réside dans les vents et reste au centre de tous les palmiers et chaque grain de sable du conscience de quelque petit déchiré de la mer...*" "*This magnificent island where the reflections of the sun still give the water images of sea waves persisting in Thales' voice, which resonates each resounding dawn interwoven in the winds resting in the midpoint of palm trees and in each minuscule sand grain of the tear's vigilant mind of the ocean...*"

John thought about the ethnic diversity of Puerto Rico as he was proofreading an article he had just finished revising for the *San Juan Star*, the only English newspaper on the island. It catered to Americans living in their *colonias* insulated and detached intellectually from the Puerto Rican society, many of whom had lived on the island for forty years or more, without the desire to acculturate completely by learning Spanish. As a result, many North Americans remain as *outsiders* on the island, which is indicative in a small scale of the United States' waning influence in the world as a global leader due to its monolingualism. Even though a greater number of Americans are becoming more multilingual, the majority is not. This translates into the United States' singled-sided view when it pertains to foreign policy and international affairs.

The play *Vejigantes*, written by Francisco Arriví, was debuting in San Juan for the first time in ten years, and John's boss wanted him to write a story about the play. It was the first of several dramatic interpretations and musicals taking place during the first week of June in commemoration of Puerto Rican arts and culture. John was very interested in Arriví, who was still alive, because he introduced and wrote about some of the racial and ethnic taboos of Puerto Rican society in his theatrical representations. Arriví stressed the importance of the historical-political-racial syncretism of the island's society. In his opinion, many Puerto Ricans preferred to ignore their multifarious racial make-up formed by the miscegenation of the Spanish, Taíno, and African ethnic groups because, for some ridiculous reason, they believed the "white" element of Spanish and European ethnicities was superior to the others. Many vehemently denied their Black ancestry, and Arriví conveyed this racial negation in his works to help his people accept and embrace with pride their complete heritage in an attempt to educate and reduce the racism in Puerto Rican society.

Unfortunately, racism is a reality prevalent in all countries, as evidenced recently by Lance, at Gold's Gym at the *Quarry*, a predominantly Anglo shopping center for the elite in an upscale neighborhood in San Antonio, Texas. Although this is a minor incident, it is representative of how racism is manifested. That morning Lance was working out when he realized by looking through a window from the gym that he had parked in a corner space, which was blocking the accessibility of a disposal truck from unloading the garbage canister from the Fleming's Steakhouse Restaurant. Therefore, he quickly gathered his gym bag and asked the young Mexican-American lady at the front desk if he could leave his bag there temporarily while he moved his truck. She amiably agreed, and when he returned after moving his vehicle, he realized he had left his water bottle in his truck. Upon informing the young lady of his return to the parking lot a second time, she indicated that the gym policies restricted anyone from leaving their equipment there. Lance grabbed his bag returning to his truck and retrieving his water bottle; then, proceeded to come back to finish his workout. When entering the gym for the third time, he responded in Spanish, since he was slightly upset: "Aquí tienes mi tarjetita de miembro". (Here is my membership card.)

Immediately, she reported the incident to her manager accusing him of cursing her in Spanish. The manager, another Mexican-American lady, asked Lance to leave the gym assuming her associate was correct because Spanish was spoken. Neither one of the young women spoke Spanish, nor could they comprehend why Lance was speaking this foreign language to them in a predominantly Anglo commercial center. This reaction is typical of many Mexican-Americans in San Antonio who vehemently resent Mexicans or Hispanics speaking Spanish to them. Here is an example of what Arriví, the Puerto Rican dramatist, would refer to as a denial of one's true identity, in this case, the two Mexican-American women. One would think it was common for Mexican-Americans to want to embrace and honor their dual identity by becoming completely bilingual in both English and Spanish, but lamentably, the opposite is true in many cases.

Unfortunately, racism transcends borders as evidenced in Mexico, for example, where Afro-Mexicans are derided on one of the cards, *El negrito (the little Black one)*, of a popular Mexican bingo game. In another instance, Peña Nieto, the current White-Mexican president of Mexico belonging to the *Partido Revolucionario Independentista* (PRI), which has ruled the country for approximately eighty years by means of corruption, fraud, and *la mordida* (literally translated as "the bite," but meaning the payoff). The PRI would never allow an Afro-Mexican or an Aborigine-Mexican to run for president in Mexico due to the country's strong racism against darker skinned Hispanics, primarily among the elite but also predominant in Mexican society overall, especially regarding Blacks as an inferior race with limited intellectual capabilities.

Moreover, Mexico has suffered greatly under the corrupt elections and leadership of Peña Nieto and the former political leaders of the PRI, who have directly and indirectly supported the drug cartels and major narcotic traffickers, like el Chapo. When ring leaders like el Chapo are incarcerated in Mexico to give the impression that the government is doing something to combat the distribution of illegal drugs like marijuana, cocaine, and heroine, they are treated in the penitentiary as hotel guests with access to fine dining, women, movies, and all the amenities of law-abiding citizens.

They are like Jesús Malverde, the "narco-saint" born in Sinaloa, Mexico who killed his opposition and gave money to the poor and Catholic churches *en el nombre de Dios* (in God's name). He was eulogized in many of the musical corridas as fighting the corruption of the ruling PRI that stole from the poor to enrich the political elite, which was racially of a whiter European descent. Inadvertently, this chronic extortion is facilitated by its North American neighbor, the United States, a country indifferent to the nuances of Mexican politics due to its inability to speak Spanish, especially at the presidential level. This gives leverage to leaders like Mr. Nieto, who can manipulate his position by blaming the proliferation of the Mexican cartels primarily on the United States, since this American country consumes most of the drugs sold illegally. His argument becomes more convincing, since, in many cases, Mexican presidents speak fluent English and many of them have been educated in Ivy League universities, such as Harvard, like Carlos Salinas de Gortari, one of the most corrupt former PRI presidents of Mexico, who stole and deposited in his personal bank accounts millions of pesos from the country's National Treasury.

Agreeing with Arriví's meditations on racial diversity, John knew Puerto Ricans would never elect a governor like the United States in choosing Barack Obama, a Black man, for a second term. This is a great accomplishment, proving Americans can elect an Afro-American president overcoming the national stigma of a divided country, which has improved considerably since the Civil Rights Movement of the 1960s. Unfortunately, the complete failure of this presidency and its administration have been marred by Obama's hollow words and inactions, for example, as evidenced in Syria (2014), when he stated: "We will draw the red line against Bashar al-Assad who used chemical warheads indiscriminately against the rebels seeking to depose him of his totalitarian regime killing many children and innocent citizens." Now, the war has been lingering on for four years killing some 220,000 people and creating a worldwide refugee problem for displaced Syrians. Not only has Obama's policies failed internationally, but they have left an African-American community with higher unemployment rates along with an increase in violent crimes and murders, primarily among Blacks, in his home state of Chicago.

Obama is an American president who spends more time on talk shows with David Letterman and sporting events like the Super Bowl in an attempt to boost his image as a cool president while, for example, the numerous incidents of police brutality have blossomed, as witnessed in Ferguson, Missouri when an overzealous White police officer shot a petulant Black teenager Michael Brown for showing some emotion; when Freddie Gray, a twenty-five-year-old African-American, was arrested in Baltimore and later died after being hospitalized in a coma.

Not only have Obama's inactions led to a spree of conflicts and killings of more Blacks and White police officers across our nation in 2015, but it has also given a green light for terrorists, primarily the Islamic State, that have mushroomed in the Syrian Civil War. Their ability to cowardly spread terror has come to the forefront after kidnapping and decapitating American and foreign journalists, as well as other European citizens, and creating videos of these atrocities for the world to see via the Internet. In addition, Obama's administration drafted a nuclear arms cessation agreement with Iran, one of the most rogue countries in the world, known historically for advocating the destruction and annihilation of America. This disguised agreement benefits Iran, since economic sanctions amounting to $1.7 billion in frozen Iranian assets would be lifted. There is no doubt Iran will hide their nuclear development plants from United Nation inspectors as they have craftily done in the past.

Meanwhile, the average American immerses himself in his iPod and smart phone drowning in his own desolate narcissism. He lacks the ability to effectively comprehend international complexities due to his own global insulation since the attacks of September 11, 2001 on the Twin Towers in New York City. The former president George W. Bush predicted this onslaught of the Islamic terrorists groups in the Middle East if the American military withdrew its troops too soon. According to his beliefs, the military needed to remain and learn the language and culture of the Middle East in order to assist them in gaining control of their own government. It was a long-term commitment of the United States in proposing a plan to help the Iraqis establish their own seat of government honoring free elections and self-governing policies with a willingness to create a forum for Shiites and Sunnis to dialogue. This would help them learn to value and respect one another's differences in a nonviolent manner; the time and effort necessary for developing this type of peaceful coexistence could be not accomplished in a limited period. However, Obama has made it clear to the terrorists groups and the world of his intentions to withdraw American military forces from Iraq and Afghanistan ever since he took office seven years ago in 2009, which has given the Muslim jihadists the leverage they needed to expand and recruit more followers.

In addition, recently, due to the actions of the Obama administration the Supreme Court has ruled that a man can marry a man and a woman a woman. Wouldn't it be ludicrous at some point if a person chose to marry a woman and a man at the same time? As Albert Camus, the 20th century French existentialist and philosopher, described in his book, *La Chute*, "It is all about fornicating and enjoying the peace of solitude." However, I think he was referring only to the intercourse between a man and woman as supported by Jean-Paul Sartre, another 20th century French existentialist, in one of his stories from the book

The Wall denoting the intimacy between a man and a woman. In his story, a woman fornicates with another man, but still loves her husband who suffers from erectile dysfunction and cannot satisfy her physically.

Obama's liberal policies protect and advocate the rights of homosexuals at the expense of possibly diluting American Judeo-Christian values. Lance believes in democracy in which the voice of homosexuals and all people, regardless of race or gender, are respected, but he strongly felt like state government should determine whether homosexuals should have the legal right to marry not the federal government. Unfortunately, Obama is spineless and is more concerned about his public ratings. He posts, for example, "tweets" of educational reforms to appeal to the younger generation, who voted him into office, by proposing free tuitions for those choosing to attend junior colleges and four year universities by increasing taxes for the rich to pay for these expenses.

The painting of the famous 19th century Spanish artist Francisco Goya comes to mind, *Saturn Devouring His Son*, as Lance was thinking about American politics in the Middle East. This is a grotesque and bloody image of a dark period in Europe, one triggered by the senseless wars initiated by Napoleon Bonaparte and his French soldiers invading Spain in 1808 and indiscriminately killing innocent Spanish people and others. This encroachment, much like that of the Americans, Spanish, Russians, and other nationalities as depicted throughout history, demonstrates a lack of compassion and true respect for other cultures. This indifference is part of human nature and is predominant in all people, regardless of their nationality.

An election of an Afro-Puerto Rican governor, as mentioned previously, would never happen in Puerto Rico, or for that matter, in any other country in Latin American, Central America, or Europe. Since, as Arriví craftily pointed out in his works, there is a strong racial prejudice against Afro-Puerto Ricans on the Caribbean island which is very sad and unfortunate. He portrayed this image in his play *Vejigantes* when one of the female characters uses white powder to cover-up the *blackness* of her skin inherited from her Black grandmother, who is kept in a backroom, when an Anglo American suitor visits the granddaughter in their Puerto Rican home. As John read and proofed his completed article, he was glad he decided to move to Puerto Rico with his family because learning Spanish and living in a foreign country outside of the United States was very surreal, better than a dream, and extremely fascinating and liberating.

The Sullivan family often walked along the unsoiled beach as the tropical froth created by the waves filled the pores of the silky sand. The comforting sensation of the water soaked John's feet as they sank into the soft grainy substance. The effervescence of the water relaxed him as he frolicked aimlessly in the predawn light along the shore of the Isla Verde Beach, the most popular, if not the most sublime strip of beach in San Juan. He savored the solitude of the fresh but salty breeze, which beckoned him with its solacing call. His dark black hair was tinted with patches of gray. The shadow of his thin, but resilient physique, created by the sun disappeared in the *arena* (sand) as the ocean pounded its surface. He was born in Mercedes, Texas, an economical and culturally depressed town in South Texas, which contrasted greatly with its abundance of sunshine and fertile soil for growing grapefruit and others sumptuous fruits and vegetables. Mercedes was renown along with Brownsville as a mecca for agricultural produce. Growing up in the subtropical region of the Rio Grande Valley was a majestic experience. He remembered the freedom he often missed when, as a child, he used to ride his bicycle for countless hours through the vast and expansive farms surrounding the valley. The summer days he spent swimming with his friends in the canals fed by the Rio Grande River seemed endless.

In particular, he reminisced of one specific day at the end of May when he and Nathan, his best friend, skipped class and spent the day eating more than a half-dozen grapefruits in a field adjacent to the schoolyard. The tangy taste of the fruit did not mix well with the pack of Camel cigarettes they smoked that afternoon. They became very sick and dizzy; regretfully, they wished they had gone to school. The memory was etched away in John's mind as he remembered those spontaneous and whimsical moments. Those were the days he would always cherish; now, some of those experiences were slowly being relived in Puerto Rico as he walked along the beach.

Mexico had always intrigued John, and being near the border, he contemplated the stark differences between the two countries. Not only did the English language differ greatly from Spanish, but also, a long history united and separated the two countries, specifically Texas and Mexico. Texas and much of the Southwestern states of America had belonged to Mexico in the 16th century, and it wasn't until the mid 19th century when the first Anglo-American frontiersmen began to settle in Texas. After the U.S.-Mexican War of 1846-1848, Texas finally became part of North America. Before the war, the Catholic Church and Santa Anna, a military dictator who controlled all of the land and states of the Mexican Federation, represented the centralized Mexican government that ruled over its people. His oppressive form of government contrasted greatly with the individuality of the American settlers who wanted to purchase their own land, exercise their individual constitutional rights for freedom, and elect their government democratically. John had a keen interest in the history, specifically between the Spanish and North American cultures. For this reason, he was excited about moving to Puerto Rico, a country with Hispanic ties and distinctive cultural traits, which differed immensely from those of the United States. John was attracted to the unknown aspects of living in a foreign country where he could unearth its unique mysteries. In Mercedes, he lived on the edge of two cultures, but moving to this beautiful Caribbean island, he could live within the *labyrinth* of a new and multifarious people.

John had just arrived to San Juan with his wife Josephine and their two children, Lance and Karla. They had been in Puerto Rico for two months. Karla was five years old and Lance was three and a half. Josephine was thrilled about John's new job as a reporter for the San Juan Star, the only English newspaper on the island; however, she was apprehensive about learning Spanish and adapting to the nuances of a new culture. John spoke some Spanish, but nevertheless, he would have to brush up on this language because he spoke a little "Tex-Mex," a dialect of Spanish from the Valley in South Texas. "¡*Órale ése*!" (Hey, dude!) This was one of his favorite expressions. In high school, he was the captain of the basketball team, a lanky 6'2" power forward, averaging twenty plus points per game. John would always say, "*Dale shine a Frankenstein... Híjole*", meaning, more or less: "Let's get after it dude." "*Ésos eran los días*". (Those were the days.) John knew he could not survive solely on his broken Spanish in Puerto Rico.

During his college years, he always enjoyed reading the American Romantics: Ralph Waldo Emerson, Henry David Thoreau, Herman Melville, and Edgar Allan Poe. They wrote about nature and its stimulating effect on mankind. John envisioned the tropical beach as Thoreau's Walden Pond, a place where he could escape from the pressures of the world and lose himself in the midst of nature's renewing forces created by God. John was thirty-one years old, and he was ecstatic because he was living his dream. For ten years, he had dreamt about moving to a Latin American country; now, he and his family were in Puerto Rico—***La isla del encanto—The Enchanted Island***.

John did not hesitate to accept the job as a freelance reporter in San Juan. His dream first came to fruition when he was drafted and served in the Navy for two years, soon after marrying Josephine, and he valued this experience very much because he traveled and patrolled the Pacific Ocean with the U.S. Navy after the Korean War in the late 1950s. Unknowingly and a great bequest to him at the time for setting the course for the rest of his life, this prelude in his life proved to be one of his most valued after marrying Josephine. On tour to the Pacific Islands for two years, he remembered eating at a restaurant on one of the islands off the coast of Thailand with a group of people, all five of whom were of different nationalities speaking their individual native languages. They all circumvented the same table discussing politics, economics, and social issues as they related to their respective countries and the world at the time. The image of this evening would linger in his mind forever, since all five people were expressing their views as best they could without understanding each other's language, a kaleidoscope of divergent perspectives. Not only did John want to commit his life to his work as a reporter, but he also desired to live and become a part of the Puerto Rican society and culture to experience the excitement and *clatter* of a new adventure. Josephine was also ecstatic about going to *Borinquén*, the name given to this island by the native *Taíno* inhabitants who dwelled in this enchanted land. They both sensed it would be an invaluable experience for Lance and Karla, since they could become bilingual at an early age. This cultural exposure was very *avant-garde*, since most people preferred to remain in their native niche where everyone spoke the same language and shared the same traditions and views. This is the safe *haven*, which is natural, where most people rest and remain in their cultural comfort zone because the fear of the unknown is too overwhelming and inconceivable to most, regardless of the country they are from. John remembered reading the well-known Spanish writer-philosopher, José Ortega y Gasset, the 20th century author, who stated in his work *La rebelión de las masas*: "Soy ciudadano del mundo". (Je suis citoyen du monde… I am a citizen of the world.) These words resonated with John because he was now living the most thrilling time of his life. He never imagined relocating to Puerto Rico after leaving Mercedes on the day after graduating from high school in 1950. He carried his "own cross," so to speak, as he hitchhiked on his first journey on his way to Virginia selling bibles before attending Baylor University that fall with a scholarship to study theology and become a minister. At the time, he did not know that he would change his major to history, still remaining a strong Christian, and become a *passionate* journalist.

John thought it was necessary to go abroad and learn another language to essentially acculturate oneself in a foreign society like Puerto Rico. Reading about a country was not the same as experiencing life in that place firsthand. John strongly believed that many of the problems in the world stemmed from the ignorance emanating from the *abyss of misunderstanding*, which oftentimes divides countries and cultures. When this occurs, it is difficult for nations to interact with one another because their isolation promotes hatred and an inability to work together. This tribal condition stifles communication and separates men from each other. John wanted to comprehend this xenophobia, which afflicted all of mankind.

Before John was drafted, he was working on a graduate degree in journalism at the University of Missouri in Columbia. He met Josephine in Sunday school at the First Baptist Church in Columbia, and soon afterwards, they married and bought a house in Independence about one hundred miles west of Columbia. He would never forget Josephine's radiant smile and bright blue eyes. They were enamored *ipso facto*. As John slowly ambulated along the beach, he remembered his children looking through a window in their home in Independence. It was snowing that morning, and John felt distraught because Karla and Lance would have to spend another day cooped up inside the house. Now, his kids could play outdoors all the time in the tropical climate of the Caribbean.

In Independence John had worked for the *Kansas City Star*, and Josephine was employed as a registered nurse at the Sanitarium Hospital. Although she did not have a job lined up in San Juan, they knew it would be easy for her to find one, since there is always a demand for nurses everywhere. All of Josephine's family lived in Missouri; at first, the thought of moving to Puerto Rico was frightening. However, she was looking forward to the new experience because she had always wanted to travel and discover new places. Conversely, John was an only child, and he had a very close relationship with his parents when he was growing up; however, there was quite an age difference between them because his parents had him as older adults. His mother was a beautiful lady multitalented with a gift for serving the Lord through her God-given talents of singing and playing the piano. She also possessed a fierce independent spirit according to a banking representative Lance recently met last month in Whitesboro, a quaint small town in North Texas, where he stayed for two nights before travelling on to Guthrie, Oklahoma to compete in a triathlon. On his way back to Canyon Lake, Texas from Oklahoma, he picked up an exquisite lightly stained medium brown wood antique table he purchased at the Butterfield Stage Stop Antique Emporium located on Main Street in downtown Whitesboro. The cushions of the four chairs were redone masterfully with a roster motif by the wide eyed owner of the store, an adorable lady in her youthful 60s who partnered with her endearing husband who served in the U.S. Navy and now dedicated his time to playing cards and selling antiques. This sentimental purchase was very meaningful to Lance because his grandmother, who he met as a young child but did not remember, was born on the second floor of a striking *delicate* Victorian home with decorative wood carvings all along the exterior built in the late 19th century in this quiet town. Lance felt blessed, since he was able to roam and peruse this home in the summer of 2006 when he stopped in this town overnight on his way to Topeka, Kansas to complete in a triathlon. Afterwards, he visited his grandmother in Columbia, Missouri, who was ninety-two at the time and who passed on that December. His grandmother Edith, John's mother, unfortunately died prematurely of a cardiac arrest at the age of fifty-five, and his grandfather remarried in a few years following her demise. His new mother-in-law disliked John; therefore, he did not maintain a close relationship with his father and new wife, which saddened him for many years of his adult life.

The first three years in Puerto Rico went by very rapidly. John enjoyed his job, and he did not regret moving to San Juan. Josephine had not found a job yet, but she had an interview this week at one of the local hospitals. Karla and Lance had attended kindergarten, first, and second grades at one of the many private North American schools on the island. Even though the children were getting a decent education, John and Josephine were not satisfied because they were not learning Spanish. John was strongly opposed to them only learning English and associating with North American children, since they were presently living in a Hispanic country. It would be a difficult and painful transition; however, he strongly believed it was important to enroll Karla and Lance in Spanish speaking schools only.

After inquiring about the public school system, John matriculated Lance and Karla in a Spanish public school named Julio Sellés Solá, one of the model public schools on the island. Lance remembered his first day of school. Everyone looked different, they had an olive-skinned color (trigueño), and their hair and eyes were considerably darker than his. The older seventh and eighth grade girls were attracted to Lance's blond hair and blue eyes. Not only was Lance befuddled by the stark differences between himself and the other students, but he was also very confused and dazzled daily because he could not understand anything his teacher or the other students were saying. The transition and adjustment period was quite intense for a third grader.

During the first couple of weeks Mrs. Rodríguez, Lance's spelling teacher, would ask Lance to stay in the classroom every day for 15 minutes during their lunch hour. She would review the Spanish alphabet with him, and she would help him pronounce Spanish words correctly. Lance was very thankful for her love and compassion for teaching as he distinctly recalled her diligence in helping him reiterate the vocalic word: "Aeropuerto—A—E—R—O—P—U—E—R—T—O." What a wonderful teacher! Aeropuerto means airport, which was very coincidental on numerous levels, because not only did the word contain the majority of the Spanish vowels, but also later in life he became enamored with travelling and still enjoys visiting other countries.

Karla had similar experiences, and it was not long before she began speaking Spanish fluently as well. Karla read voraciously and excelled in every subject. Not only was she very bright, but she also established a good rapport with her teachers and friends at school. Josephine and John were very proud of the progress their children were making in school.

In the fifth and sixth grades, Lance became more contumacious and rebellious. He enjoyed spending most of his time outside. The older boys at school often connived Lance into picking fights with other boys in the schoolyard, but most of the time, many Puerto Rican boys wanted to fight him, since he was the only Anglo student around. Watching the younger kids fight was a source of entertainment for the older boys. This was part of a ritual, which all boys would experience to make the transition from boyhood to manhood. In Puerto Rican society, it was an unprecedented *rite of passage* to prove one's masculinity in front of others to gain their acceptance and approval, a cultural value termed *el machismo*. The older guys would often help defend Lance if he could not hold his own with bigger boys his age who wanted to bully him, especially, since their girlfriends enjoyed touching his silky blond hair. He was not a threat to them because he was still too young to "steal" their girlfriends, so to speak, from them. Sometimes Lance would need a slight advantage by striking bigger boys with his nickel plated belt buckle.

Lance repeated this phrase, his "war" chant to himself before fighting: "¡Los hombres valientes son victoriosos!" (Brave men are victorious!) Lance knew there was no turning back now. It all happened one day when Lance was standing in line to eat lunch at the school cafeteria and a boy in back of him shoved him. Lance looked back and noticed it was Anselmo, a big seventh grader. Anselmo laughed and said, "¿Qué pasa? ¡Pendejo!" (What's your problem? Asshole!) Lance did not hesitate to throw a punch, which only grazed Anselmo's angular but bony face. The other students standing in line grabbed the two boys and separated them. Lance retorted, "Me cago en tu madre. ¡Cabrón!" (I defecate on your mother. Mother fucker!) At that point Lance knew he had crossed the line, and he would have to confront this jerk later that afternoon or on the following day. Anselmo had a reputation for picking on smaller guys. Lance agonized the rest of the day, and his palms were very sweaty. He wondered how this one would turn out. However, he knew it was important to defend his honor, a Puerto Rican cultural nuance he had instinctively acquired through *osmosis* now that he was a sixth-grader. A man's honor in Puerto Rican society is everything. Lance wanted to fit into this unknown world; therefore, he felt pressured to react accordingly.

Nothing happened the rest of the day, but rumor had it Anselmo was going to beat the crap out of Lance. Everyone seemed to be gearing up for the big fight. All of Lance's older friends told him not to worry because Anselmo was a big wimp. They knew he lived with his mother, and he had to be a fag, a common judgment during the 1970s. How could a woman raise a real man? Rumor had it that Anselmo's father was a homosexual who hung out in *Old San Juan*, the old section of town decorated with cobble stone streets and Spanish verandas filled with an abundance of lush bougainvillea with their peach, purple, and red buds interwoven perfectly with the white washed stucco of the homes adorned with red and white hibiscus flowers. Many of the *casas* (homes) had open roofed patios in their epicenters where lazy water flowed from a fountain surrounded by luscious green philodendrons and palms radiating gleefully in the beams of the tropical sun. A person could sit for hours in such a place where the smell of the salt from the Caribbean Sea permeated through the air carrying the distant echo of *salsa* (the authentic genre of Puerto Rican music) by Tito Puente and the band *El Gran Combo*, emanating from a radio someone was carrying along narrow streets. Streets frequented by the historical memories of Juan

Ponce de León, the first Spanish governor of the island in 1509. And, if one listened silently enough, it was possible to hear the lethargic waves from the Atlantic crashing methodically on the rocks protecting the Northeastern seaboard of San Juan's Bay where *footprints* of Christopher Columbus and the pirates, Frances Drake and John Hawkins, with a multitude of other Spanish conquistadors lived ubiquitously in the endless tunnel of time. The *mélange* of sounds, smells, and scenery were not only seductive and sensual, but also very intoxicating. Rumor had it that someone saw Anselmo's father and another man copulating one night on one of the street corners in Old San Juan near *El Batey*, a popular bar. The bad thing about this disgusting act between two men was that his father was the subservient participant who yelled: "¡Métemelo!" (Screw me!) As Lance grew older, he realized that it was common to fabricate rumors and to aggrandize them to such a hyperbolic state that most stories were incredulous. In any event, Lance's friends reassured him they would back him up if there was a need. Lance did not totally trust them, since they never had a reason to follow through with their promises because he had always come out on top. Nevertheless, instinctively, he knew his streak of good luck would not continue forever.

At school the next day everything seemed normal. The first bell rang at ten till eight, and everyone was seated in their classrooms by 8 a.m. Mrs. Vélez, Lance's Spanish teacher, noticed that Lance was unusually quiet this morning contrasting sharply with his normally jovial and loquacious demeanor. "¿Todo está bien esta mañana Lance?" (Is everything all right this morning Lance?)

"Sí, todo está bien. No dormí muy bien anoche porque estaba terminando una tarea para mi clase de historia". (Yes, everything is fine. I just didn't sleep very well last night because I stayed up late finishing some homework for my history class.) Lance knew she was suspicious about something because she always seemed cognizant of what was going on. Her nickname was la *Vieja Loba* (Old Wolf) because she was very intuitive and knew when the *shit was going to hit the fan*.

At ten o'clock sharp, the bell rang for the mid-morning break called *La merienda*, the regular snack time. Lance jumped out of his seat and began walking outside. Normally, he would walk over to *la tiendita* (the little store) to buy some candy, baseball cards, a *límber* (frozen flavored ice in a cup), some *coquito* (fresh coconut) ice cream, *quenepas* (a refreshing native fruit), or *churros* (deep fried dough sprinkled with sugar). The children also savored the indelible *pastelillos de fresas, queso o carne* (small fried fritters filled with strawberries, cheese, or meat). However, his favorite candy was *el ajonjolí*, a small squared cluster of sesame seeds covered with light caramel syrup. On the way there, he saw Anselmo and a couple of his friends waiting for him in the middle of the street in between the schoolyard and *la tiendita*. Anselmo spoke first, "Oye, pendejito. Ahora voy a partirte esa carita de gringuito en dos". Basically, he said he was going to kick his ass and smash his *gringo* face. *Gringo* was a term with many etymological origins, one derived by the South Texas cowboys and American soldiers, who wore green uniforms. They pursued Pancho Villa in Mexico during the Mexican Revolution after he crossed the *Río Bravo* and raided the small town of Columbus, New Mexico on March 9, 1916. The native Mexicans would see the American soldiers dressed in green, and derisively tell them: "Green go... home." Therefore, the term *gringo* evolved, also a derivative of the word "Greek" used in the idiomatic expression: "He must be speaking Greek." In other words, one could not understand their language because they were foreigners. Mexicans also used the term gringo during the U.S.-Mexican War of 1846-1848 when referring to the American soldiers.

As Lance approached him, he began to unfasten his belt. Anselmo was bigger than he was; therefore, he decided he needed a little extra advantage. Then Lance replied, "Tu madre es una puta". After calling his mother a whore, Anselmo came charging at Lance. Lance took one step backwards and swung his nickel belt buckle, which struck him on the right temple. Blood began gushing as Anselmo grabbed his head with both hands. Blood splattered down the side of his face and covered his shirt collar. Anselmo's friends were startled as to what had just happened. They were petrified and tried to grab Lance, but he took off running. He knew he could outrun them, especially with the extra adrenaline surging through his body.

Meanwhile, Lance ran through the neighborhood for about two miles. He could no longer hear footsteps behind him, perceiving he was finally alone enjoying a very comforting solitude. His thoughts were so clear and pure, and this *state of mind* was later underscored in his life by Thich Nhat Hanh, the Vietnamese Buddhist spiritual leader of the 21st century, who stated clearly in many of his works: "One must suffer to find his/her own happiness. Suffering and happiness coexist in each breath and moment of life." Instinctively, Lance was alone in his fear and suffering, but the presence of God was revealed to him in the field of tall grass where his soul was restored and refreshed by the light breeze and soft sun beaming down on him in his *juncture* of isolation and joy, a field of ecstatic jubilance emanating from within. There was an empty field about 200 yards in front of him. The tall grass in the middle of the field was swaying in the wind, and to the right there was a small crop of sugar cane. He wondered if the *Taíno* Indians felt the same sense of relief when they evaded the attacks of the Spaniards in the 16th century. This moment was ethereal, and he would remember the tranquility forever. The adrenaline must have purged his body, and its effect saturated him with an overwhelming calmness. He would spend the rest of the day here amid the *prado* (meadow) and his thoughts. He felt bad about hitting Anselmo with his belt buckle, but he did not think about this feeling of guilt for long. He only listened to his surroundings and thoughts, which echoed in his mind by vociferating softly: "I feel very calm and secure now. The green grass, the breeze, and radiant sun are my true friends. I don't have to prove myself to them. They exist and seem to accept me just as I am. At this school I often have to defend my manhood. I know I am a *gringo* with blue eyes and blond hair, and I don't really fit into this cultural environment. The fighting must be an expression of this racial conflict between me and the other Puerto Rican boys. However, the only thing that matters right now is this point in time."

As he closed his eyes and listened to the wind, he heard his internal voice speaking again: "We spend so much time thinking and worrying about our present condition, which is oftentimes miserable and incomprehensible, rather than focusing on the positive aspects of our present life, the here and now of the present moment. Life passes us by so quickly. Our routine, activities, and battles engulf our every waking hour. We have to pull ourselves from these activities and responsibilities to listen, hear, touch, feel, and see our surroundings. Once we stop and take time to be alive, we truly know and sense our purpose, which is to be one with nature, mankind, and ourselves. This remains unknown to man until he separates himself from society and others. When he is truly alone with nature, he begins to comprehend." After several hours of silent contemplation, Lance returned to school. It was almost 3 p.m., and Josephine would pick him and Karla up at the northeastern corner of the school perimeter.

Lance endured many fights that year. In a strange way, they were adventurous, and he liked the attention and acceptance he gained from his peers and older friends. Proving one's masculinity and courage were very important traits to demonstrate in the schoolyard. Everyone looked up to and accepted Lance because he was not afraid to fight. Fighting helped him fit into this bizarre and unknown "macho" world. He could not fully understand the changes he was experiencing: learning a new language and eating unfamiliar food (rice, beans, plantain [plátano] dishes, such as mofongo, amarillos, and tostones; lechón [spiked smoked pig cooked in a slow burning pit in the ground], cuchifrito [deep fried pork ears and tails], and morcillas [a blood type sausage]) along with assimilating the new values (masculinity and aggressiveness) of the Puerto Rican society, especially among the males. In addition, one could not overlook the coveted *Bacardí rum*, one of the best rums in the world distilled on the island.

The following years were just as venturesome for Lance although he had difficulty determining who he was. He remained confused about his identity. At home he spoke English and ate goulash (a special dish consisting of macaroni noodles, tomato sauce, ham, and hamburger meat) with his family; at school he spoke Spanish and ate *arroz con pollo* (rice and chicken). These opposing environments really confused him. Even when he defecated, the smell was different depending on whether he ate the *goulash* at home or the *tostones* at the school cafeteria. He often asked himself, "Am I a Puerto Rican or a North American? What is the difference and should I be concerned about it?" He did not want to ignore this conflicting problem.

In the sixth grade, Lance became very interested in sports. He always completed his schoolwork; however, he spent more time outdoors running and shooting a basketball. Sports provided an escape from the difficulties he was experiencing fighting and searching for his identity. That year he remembered participating in the annual field day, a series of track and field events, which the school organized once a year. This year the sixth and seventh-graders would compete against the eighth-graders. Lance had trained and practiced for two months. He conditioned himself to run the 200, 400, and 800-meter races.

John and Josephine were very excited about Lance's zeal for sports. John had been an athlete during his high school days in Mercedes, Texas where he played football, basketball, baseball, soccer, and tennis as a youngster, and he excelled as the captain of the varsity basketball team his senior year. His team, the Mercedes Tigers, was runner up in the 1950 State Championship Basketball Tournament in the 2-A division. Later, when John attended Baylor University in Waco, Texas, he lamented never trying out for the basketball team. After denying himself that opportunity and regretting it immensely, John would never sell himself short in the future, whether a new door opened for work or later in life when he would dedicate his life to God, Josephine, and his children. He would neither ignore his passion as a writer of political-cultural novels correlated directly to the French and Spanish Caribbean islands, Latin America, France, Montreal, and other countries as they interacted internationally with the United States. This strong conviction proved to be true when he asked Josephine to marry him on their third date, and he *scampishly* gave her a twenty-four-hour ultimatum. Once they married, their decision to move to Puerto Rico leaving behind family and a known culture was decisive. He shared his feelings with his son: "Never resolve not to participate in sports or any other activity because you think you are not good enough. It's the effort you put out that counts." John learned it is much harder to live knowing you did not try something than to have tried and failed.

As John watched his son prepare for competition at the baseball field, which was converted as best as possible into a track in Villa Nevárez, the residential area where the school was located, he remembered Plato's famous words: "The due proportion of mind and body is the loveliest and fairest sight to him/her who has a seeing eye." The quote was memorialized in John's mind forever. He had been reading Plato's *Republic* when he ran across this quote, which has influenced him over the years. He always acknowledged the interrelationship between the mind, body, and spirit along with academics and sports, and Plato's words expressed this relationship perfectly.

John would often lose himself in reflection as he thought about history and the progression of cultures and ideas throughout time, from the Middle Ages to the present. He reveled in reading Georg Wilhelm Friedrich Hegel, a German philosopher from the 18th-19th centuries, who stated that "universal reason" is the most important aspect of life. Man should not only search within to find his inner truth and values, but he should also probe the world through the eyes of history, so that the truth of all men and societies may be revealed. John believed life was very brief, and there was not enough time to *absorb* everything it had to offer. But because of the brevity of man's existence, he wanted to take advantage of his "space" to learn and live life to its fullest. There was no time in his life for indolence, gossip, despair, or dissatisfaction with living. John realized all men were susceptible to many trials and tribulations, but he believed once men realized life is difficult, as expressed in the first sentence of Scott Peck's book *The Road less Travelled*, it would be easier for man to overcome adverse situations. Adversity was part of living, and the sooner one accepted this truth, the easier it would be to master the repeated *seesaw* of living. Mastery is never complete, but reminding oneself of the need to learn and relearn to refocus was fundamental. Dwelling in between the fibers of *battling* and the stable waters of tranquility is imperative because the cycle of this tension will repeat itself continuously, regardless of man's urgent obsession to control life's wavering nature. After all, it was Buddha who believed man fights his *natural condition*: "Man is supposed to get sick, grow old, and die." In our Western culture, we ignore this process of growth and decay because we don't want to suffer. We believe life is infinite when in reality it is very finite. Our Western tradition has taught us all subconsciously to crave, be selfish, and seek the impossible. Buddha suggests we should just let life run its course, and we would not succumb to these *spiritual perils*. Along this same vein, Arthur Schopenhauer, the 19th century German philosopher, believed men's desires and instincts lead him to unhappiness because the satisfaction received from a fulfilled desire leaves many unfulfilled voids. Therefore, he concluded men should not will or desire anything. In this state, one desires nothing, and this is *nirvanic asceticism*. You are at peace with yourself, since you are ignoring your desires, which are many times corrupted by society and the need of people to conform to someone else's idea of reality. In a world without an individual's will, instincts, and desires, one can truly live. Schopenhauer affirmed music to being the only art form that does not copy ideas already known to man; thus, John realized this melodic medium must have represented the only stage of our human condition for the German thinker, in which the *will* did not interfere in guiding man's corrosive attributes.

As John, Josephine, and Karla sat in the bleachers, waiting for the start of the competition, John felt the strong rays of the sun's heat evaporate the sweat on his brow cooling his forehead. A distinct stillness filled the air as the athletes and coaches prepared for the competition. The silence cushioned John's thoughts as he contemplated the beauty and serenity of the early morning. This was *joy* revealed in a fleeting moment. He remembered Robert Frost's famous verse: "Two roads diverged in the forest, and I took the one less traveled which made all the difference in the world." Moving to Puerto Rico was definitely a move most North Americans would never consider making. The Spanish language and values were disparate, the standard of living was lower, and Anglo-Saxons were definitely a minority. John and Josephine were able to look beyond the superfluous divergences to appreciate the culture and true heritage of Puerto Rico, an island rich in its unique historical civilization that could only be valued by learning Spanish and becoming a part of its community. Socrates said, "Know thyself," and John could not think of a more appropriate way of getting to know oneself other than by learning about others. After all, Socrates implied that man learned about himself when he took the time to *grasp* and comprehend others, not just in one's own country but in the world around him. John's intent on becoming part of Puerto Rican society and of the earth's macrocosm was very poignant. He wanted to experience more than just everyday living and going through the motions of life without questioning its innate spirit.

Josephine and Karla began to cheer as Lance prepared himself along with the other runners to run the 200-meter dash. John sat anxiously waiting for the start of the race. He had always supported Lance encouraging him to embrace the value of competition, but he also emboldened Lance to enjoy himself. Winning was fun, but the true lesson of sports was to espouse and savor the effort, whether in victory or defeat. Competing to the best of one's inherent ability underscores the essence not just of sports, but everything in life. When the contest becomes the Chinese yin yang or balance of existence, one is truly alive and free. The starter gathered all of the competitors together with their various colored T-shirts. The eighth-graders were cladded in green, the seventh-graders in yellow, and the sixth-graders in blue. The conditions for running were perfect, since the wind was slightly blowing with a bright sun and its soft warmness gleaming on the young athletes.

The starting gun sounded, and Lance felt his heart leap to his throat as he surged forward, pumping his arms and lifting his legs as hard and as fast as possible. The lactic acid built up rapidly in his extremities with each stride. This was a new sensation, one which he had not experienced before. The noise and excitement of the crowd was exhilarating, an overwhelming elation. Josephine, Karla, and John were standing in the bleachers cheering for Lance and the other participants. Lance finished the race in third place with a time of thirty-five seconds overcoming the daunting efforts of four other competitors. John smiled with satisfaction as he watched his son pick up the green third place ribbon and relished in all the young students who gave forth their best effort.

Lance had less than ten minutes to prepare himself for the 400-meter dash. He and his friend Roberto were the favorites in this race. Concurrently, the starter fired the gun, and ten runners jostled for position running the first loop around the outer perimeter of the baseball field. Lance surged into the lead pursued closely by Roberto and the other young boys. Lance controlled his breathing and ran conservatively, knowing he had to run two laps. Slowly, Roberto and Lance began to pull away from the pack of runners, and they finished the first lap toe to toe. Then, effortlessly, Roberto extended his lead incrementally as Lance tried to narrow the gap; purposely, his opponent's superior effort left Lance somewhat discouraged but content.

With 100 meters to go, Lance put on a kick and almost passed Roberto, but efficiently, his friend had enough in his reserve to accelerate and beat him by two seconds.

Clutching desperately for big gulps of air, Lance tried to regain his breath. He could hear his family and other spectators cheering in the stands as his consciousness faded temporary, a splendorous moment never forgotten to this day. Nevertheless, he only had fifteen minutes to prepare for the following 800-meter run, one in which he would join Roberto again along with six other youngsters coursing four laps around the circumference of the baseball field. The javelin throw, the long jump, and high jump were all taking place simultaneously while Lance concentrated and regained his composure for his next event. Lance was not aware of it now, but later on in life, he would look back at this day reminiscing about it often. Not only was this the beginning of a love for disciplining and training his body, but he was also relishing and coping with the emotional newness of competing with others. But of more significance, he was learning about the challenges he would face throughout life: the ups and downs, victories and defeats, and realities and fantasies of one's conscious and unconscious mind. Years later, he read Miguel de Unamuno, the late 19th century Spanish writer and philosopher, who wrote, "La vida es lucha, y la lucha es vida". (Life is a struggle, and the struggle is life.) Now, Lance mused more wisely over these words because he had many more experiences, good and bad, to add to the scar tissue of his existence, realizing we all live in this Unamunian continuum.

Lance and the others jockeyed for position at the starting line. The ubiquitous shriek sounded again thrusting the runners forward in fluid motion. Lance felt a little bleary, since his breathing was irregular and tense; in a moment of déjà vu, he was trailing behind Roberto again. Everyone finished the first lap together with three laps to go, and Lance was presently feeling the debilitating fatigue of the previous events. His wobbly arm swing drained him, and his strides were noticeably choppy and uncoordinated. Even though he was light-headed, he combatted to not lose sight of Roberto, instinctively, holding on to the interminable pace and withstanding the pain. As they jetted into the last 100 meter stretch, Roberto kicked and pulled away leaving everyone behind. Lance tried to sprint in vain as his arms and legs were laboriously working to diffuse the lactic acid buildup, but his delirious mind only thought about crossing the finish line where he collapsed upon traversing. Ecstatically, unaware of Lance's condition, John, Josephine, and Karla jumped to their feet. The officials quickly embraced and lifted Lance up from the ground and helped him walk. Slowly with each breath and step, he regained consciousness and the refreshing taste of water revived his depleted constitution; thus, he reveled in the euphoria of dopamine filtering through his limbs after he returned physically to his homeostatic state. This *existential panacea* would be an elixir his addictive persona craved daily as exercise and its benefits formed a habit he could not forego for the remainder of his adolescence and adulthood.

As Lance recouped from the run, he tried to remember how he felt. Pushing his body to the limit left him feeling as if he had entered another level of *raison d'être*. The pain he experienced was so harrowing and piercing that he sensed entering a subconscious zone bordering life and death. Once the physical agony had abated, he experienced a certain ecstasy. The incertitude of this sensation epitomized the doubtfulness of life. Man is unaware of life after death; however, he claims to be cognizant of life before death. Dante Alighieri, a premier Italian poet from the 13th-14th centuries, must have struggled with the meaning of life and death as he described the different levels of death, beginning with purgatory and ending with the final inferno. What is the attraction and need man has to apprehend the essence of the unknown? Nevertheless, Lance knew running would become an instrumental part of his life because it was an activity that allowed him to reach a level of speculation in which he could enter into the marrow of life's enigmatic corpus where he could intuit and celebrate its mysteries.

Running became puzzling to Lance because when he looked back at this day, which took place more than forty-six years ago, he pondered its relevance. The effort he put forth then and the continued resolve he manifests as a triathlete today are still the same. It was no greater at that time than it is now; therefore, Schopenhauer was right when he observed that men are not satisfied with their accomplishments. Lance had done well in many races and triathlons throughout the years, but the void within him as well as in all people is endless. This abyss thirsted to be replenished constantly not because of the necessity to overcome others in competition, but as a means to satisfy our human urgency to move, think, rest, and repeat this cycle. Lance knew life was like a puzzle, and there is a motivation to order its pieces. The exertion of exercise created pain and comfort, two complimentary components juxtaposing thought, stimulation, and meaning, which thus renew the soul. Pain was a constant indicator that inadvertently made him feel alive. The sense of completion and the titillating euphoria of being were fundamental for creating a daily space of nonbeing, a place where do you like "one" or "a person" temporarily forgets his sentient self. This insatiable passion to exercise and expend oneself physically as opposed to the propensity of comfort and leisure sublimely dictated to us by a lethargic and technocratic society is *the path less chosen*. It is also the *road* which provokes the most contemplation, a state of being most rejected by people's oblivious neglect to turn within or *ensimismarse*, a term coined by the Spanish 20th century author José Ortega y Gasset.

Man has a mind which is connected directly to his physical and spiritual being. Life without thought would be meaningless, since cerebration is derived from one's natural urgency to *be* which is completely spontaneous. When the body is exerting itself and involved in movement, it is pliable, free, and relaxed. In this state, the spirit rests in its *perfect dwelling* where it does not desire further satisfaction. Nevertheless, an excess of movement and exertion can deplete the body and can also rid the athlete of his instinctual need for reflection, the *key* that opens the door to his well-being and fountain of motivation.

Each culture has its traditions and customs which propel people to act, think, and be. In America, people are compelled to succeed monetarily which is based exclusively on performance. People want to live the dream by becoming wealthy, believing riches will provide the security, happiness, and approval by others they are taught to crave and emulate by the mega media campaign bombarding Americans from the time of conception until death with images of success.

In cultures we become entrapped with the norm's definition of life, one that strongly contradicts individual ruminations and individuality. As a result, the value of hard work, a very good trait for excelling in this type of capitalistic system, should be balanced with every individual's need for solitude, where one can tap into one's uniqueness. The more arduously one works, the more money one generates for self to purchase food, clothing, shelter, and opportunities for one's family. Oftentimes, we lose ourselves in the exterior veneer of living represented metaphorically in the multimillion homes we reside in and the multiple Porsches and other luxurious symbols that fill our garages and homes. These represent the *toys* for others to see and covet when we invite them to our cocktail parties with jazz tunes in the background. The bow ties, high heels, and tight fitting dresses of elegance displayed on our *ego's platter* are there for other's to sample. We become entrapped and enslaved to nationalistic traditions that define us instead of one delineating our individual *culture* of purpose to receive for self and give to others.

But more importantly, knowing and honoring that quiet space within, pleading with us all to listen, meditate, and allow God to carry us, is imperative for becoming cognizant that his gracious *footprints* always lift and hoist us through our pains and sufferings. We should never suppress these areas with medication and other barbiturates that temporarily relieve and dull with nonspiritual chemicals our anguishing hearts. When man accepts his *fragility* and vulnerability and submits his life to Jesus Christ and his Father, who is God to all men, in Lance's heart exclusively, he becomes free. Then, man can open his mind first to self and God as he practices his *mantra* daily within the confines of his particular culture, whether it is in the United States or China, for example.

When man *knows* himself as advocated by Socrates, he maintains his spiritual and emotional intellectual equilibrium in the global arena. As a result, he develops a *nonjudgmental* attitude towards other societies in which people speak multiple languages and practice, knowingly or purposefully: Nihilism, Buddhism, Taoism, Islamism, Judaism, Christianity, Hinduism, Confucianism, Atheism, and many other numerous religions and philosophies. Personally, Lance knew that he was not and never will be Jesus Christ; therefore, he could never judge others although he wholeheartedly believed Christ was the only master of his life and others in our global community. He could always safely speak and dwell with Jesus, through his holy spirit, in his quiet moments of solitude. Lance also understood and trusted that only God and his Son Jesus Christ would judge the world and those who did not adhere to their words and teachings. Furthermore, Lance could only love others, who worshipped differently and who even believed in a godless world, and share with them his convictions only when the relationship allowed for a peaceful nonjudgmental give and take. He often pondered and recalled Mother Teresa's infamous words: "If we were all truly Christians, there would be no Hindus in the world." Actions carried out by one's faith always speak louder than words. This was exemplified later in life when Lance would befriend Daniel, a competitive athlete and friend who was also a self-proclaimed Atheist. Through his actions, however, Daniel was more ethical than many Christians whose talk did not match their walk.

Man is meant to exist, so he can establish his sense of being and self-worth to an individual's faith who is unique but also a human being. He must develop compassion for the sufferings of others without seeking the dream of wealth exclusively because this is when society starts to decay. In this materialistic state, one loses himself blindly in his own petulant arrogance, and he severs his relationship with others. Selfish abundance separates us from ourselves and others because most people live within the confines of their own *ego*, constantly competing against others instead of embracing the brotherhood and unity of all men. Death should be the *fulcrum* that helps us view life as the dew that appears in the early morning, but that dissipates soon after the sun rises. By using this simple visual metaphor as a guide, one realizes that generating money for self is good as long as it is used to help others, once one's individual needs are met.

Sometimes education is valued only for its potential earning power, which empowers the individual with the ability to support oneself financially, but it often fails to enlighten our thirst to satiate the human soul. As Schopenhauer says, "Our desires are never satisfied." For the most part, Americans generally have enough money, yet our federal deficit and budget are in shambles because we are an insatiable nation always wanting and lusting for more. We often tell ourselves that life can be better, and the positive societal *gurus* remind us of our need to remain in an affirmative state of being. In reality life can only improve when we accept the fact that everyone ages, sickens, and dies. We are dying in the midst of life; nevertheless, we refuse to acknowledge this simple law of nature convincing ourselves of our inconceivable quest through science to conquer death and find the *fountain of deathlessness*. We live in a fictitious reality by assuming the federal budget can be balanced while our nation throws itself in the abyss of materialism. Our people avoid the unequivocal balance of redefining life within the context of its brevity for all; thus, we become philosophically more pragmatic and less spiritual not only in solving financial matters, but also in resolving the inner turmoil within each one of us.

America needs a new philosophical awakening by returning to the essence of living. Life is not about the self, who merely does his own thing, but about participating and cooperating with others. We can engage each other, at times, by being more playful, and this frivolity can free us to think more clearly and unobtrusively. Education should stimulate us to be more compassionate, less corrupt, and more interested in the interrelationship of all knowledge (science, business, art, music, literature, etc.) These disciplines are not separate but are parts of the whole, since the human condition is one. We are doomed because the balance between work and play is lost. It is through this free abandon of thought that we are most creative, free, alert, and alive. Work dulls our senses because we become slaves to society's thrust to secure the mighty dollar. This modern metaphysical heterodoxy is unrelenting and intrusive. It weakens us because it tears away at our *spirituality* and our *inner being*. We crave for the externals of life: sex, violence, material things, technology, information, and instant gratification; thus, we gain a painless existence which contrarily leads to more suffering. Yet, we ignore our internal world: the quiet solitude of an early morning sun's awakening; the exertion of a run along soft sand on an endless sleeping beach; the silent contemplation of the changing nuances of the day's light as it passes us by unnoticed; and the quiet moments of freeing ourselves from the chores our conscious minds force upon us.

When the flow of ideas is stifled by the aggrandizement of the thinker, we become lost and forget our significance. Professors, writers, journalists, and philosophers write in order to get tenure, to publish, to become someone, and to make a living, understandably. Oftentimes, writers don't exercise their craft for its inherent *joie de vivre*, the fountain of purity and unaffected musings that only are derived from the human heart. Lance would experience this lack of joy among many professors when, later in life, he would enroll in the PhD program in Spanish Literature at the University of Texas in Austin. There, he experienced the cesspool of political favoritism and ineptitude for teaching demonstrated by many of the professors, who were stuck in their mindless and unforgiving race to publish. They greedily disregarded the fundamental responsibility of giving and inspiring students in a more soulful and integrated approach to education. Many strangled themselves in their poisonous egotism ignoring their obligation to become citizens of the world as José Ortega y Gasset would admonish them to be. As global participants, sharing, enriching, and enabling each student to succeed should become the unquestionable focus and not individual greed and advancement at the demise of others. Professors, especially, should propagate this maxim for their students and audience as they create an academic holistic philosophy for everyone.

John and Josephine were very proud of Lance since he had received two second and one third place ribbons on a day Lance would never forget. During the seventh grade, Lance did very well in school. He enjoyed all of his classes, specifically his science class. His class notes were very meticulous and orderly since he rewrote them every day after returning home from school. That year he studied photosynthesis, and he liked his teacher Ms. Johnson very much. She was from Iowa, and she had been teaching at his Spanish public school, Julio Sellés Solá, for two years now. She was participating in a teacher exchange program, which promoted travel and cultural development and awareness of other countries for its participants. Ms. Johnson was very enthusiastic, and she was very glad to be in Puerto Rico where she could learn the Spanish language well.

Meanwhile, Karla was in the ninth grade, and she was an excellent student. She learned Spanish quickly because she was a very studious and assiduous child. Not only did she excel in academics, but she also belonged to the Brownies and Girl Scouts where she became very amiable and gregarious. Everyone liked her very much. Besides being an exceptionally good learner, her attractive long dark brown hair and round green eyes were very becoming. Other than reading and studying, Karla enjoyed swimming and playing tennis, two extracurricular activities that complemented her academic achievements. John and Josephine were very proud of her since she maintained a balance between her schoolwork and social interests.

During his adolescent years, Lance learned quite a bit about the Puerto Rican culture. The habits and customs of the children were very different and atypical from those he learned at home and among his English speaking friends. Lance would only realize how bizarre things were when he was older and had an opportunity to look back and reflect upon his experience on this idyllic island. For instance, if a boy would intentionally touch another boy's face, a blatant action of disrespect and dishonor, it was expected that the *"muchacho"* boy would throw the first punch. In this Latin culture, proving one's manhood coined "el machismo" was a rite of passage for both the perpetrator and his adversary. The only way to vindicate this infringement was by fighting which had a purging effect. It allowed a kid to regain his masculinity, within the Puerto Rican context of adolescence, after being humiliated in front of his peers. Proving a man's *"machismo"* was extremely paramount in the Hispanic culture. If a boy did not defend his *maleness*, he would be labelled a *pato*, which implies he was a sissy and a queer.

Not only was touching someone's face considered contentious, but if a boy touched another's buttocks, this was also regarded as reprehensible. The humiliated kid would have to strike back, or else he would be called and treated as a *pato*. Lance did not totally comprehend the implications of these behaviors at the time, but later on in life, they made more sense to him. If a boy permitted another boy to feel his buttocks intentionally, it implied that the passive *muchacho* was effeminate and had homosexual inclinations. Homosexuals in Puerto Rico are not as widely approved of as they are in some parts of the United States and the world. Homosexuality is the worst type of behavior a man can portray in a Hispanic society because it opposes all of the macho values inbred in its culture.

Understanding homosexuality in Puerto Rico is very complex because there is a double standard involved. For instance, a man who performs a sexual act on another man is accepted by some as long as he performs the masculine role. However, a man who is indifferent or takes on the feminine role is considered to be the true homosexual. The Puerto Rican and Latin American perspective of homosexuality would make more sense to Lance later on after he had lived several years in the United States. In the U.S., people did not seem to make a distinction between the active or passive role of homosexuals.

Lance also remembered that if two boys were about to have a fight, one of the boy's friends, who was a spectator, would often place a blade of grass on contender's shoulder. The other kid would either blow or knock the piece of grass off his opponent's shoulder, and this action indicated that the aggressor (the boy who blew off the blade of grass) was ready to fight. The opponent would then be obliged to strike first. If the aggressor did not knock the straw of grass from the other boy's shoulder, he was considered a *pato* or maricón (slang for queer). Friends of the contingents would often push them and encourage them to fight. There was nothing more entertaining than a good fight in the schoolyard.

Karl Marx would have noted that fighting is representative of the eternal struggle in human nature in which there is an oppressor and an oppressed. This is most commonly seen in societies where the *bourgeoisie* dominates the proletariat classes, or the rich control the actions of the poor. However, the boys fighting were establishing who was dominant over the other. Marx would have preferred men to realize this natural instinct to dominate and oppress so as not to allow these actions to influence one other's behavior in the negative sense. A realization of these traits would allow men to control and subdue their counterparts. With this ability to subjugate these tendencies, men could learn to coexist with one another and work together instead of against each other. Wars will always be inevitable unless men restrict this inherent instinct to dominate and oppress.

In the eighth and ninth grades, Lance became more rebellious. He did not spend as much time studying because he preferred to be with his friends. In the eighth grade, he spent most of his time with Felipe and Edgar. Many times their parents would drop them off at school at 7:45 a.m., fifteen minutes before school began, and they would skip class all day. When they weren't in school, they would walk along a concrete sewer alley which was about ten feet deep. It provided adequate drainage for the city whenever there was a flood, since it rained frequently on the tropical island. The alley also served as a gateway to get to *Plaza Las Américas*, a shopping center in Hato Rey.

Lance and the other boys enjoyed the thrill of skipping class and walking along the alley because they felt totally free. They developed a sense of pride and security because the sewer was their own turf, a place where the sound of flowing water comforted them. Lance recalled the simple things they would do: throwing rocks in the water, jumping across the stream, and catching guppies with rusty tin cans. On occasions, they saw old vagabond men who would sleep, defecate, and hang out in the alley. He would never forget the words: "Mira, parece que Piloto cagó aquí otra vez". (Hey, it looks like Piloto took a shit here again.) This phrase resonated in his memory just as the image of flies feasting off this disgusting matter came to mind. Piloto, which means "Pilot," was a vagabond who would frequent this remote and hidden area. Lance could not figure out why they called him Piloto. The man had a monumental protuberance in his throat, which was very grotesque, but he did not look like an airplane or pilot. It occurred to Lance, now, that he was writing and thinking about this past experience, that maybe the protuberance looked like the nose of an airplane; he was the pilot of his own plane. Nevertheless, they always called him Piloto and threw rocks at him, something he, now, regretted doing. Piloto would always chase them in a feeble attempt to grab them, but the boys would always get away laughing the whole time. As he reminisced about these moments, he felt compassion and repented for his transgressions against this indefensible person, one who had probably always been scorned and ignored by society. He realized how harsh and unrelenting adolescents can often be.

Other than throwing rocks at Piloto, they used to go to a restaurant where they ate "bocadillos," small pressed ham and cheese sandwiches, and ordered soft drinks. Afterwards, they would go to Felipe's house, since both of his parents were at work. There, they played pool and watched T.V. until 2:00 p.m. They returned to the schoolyard by 2:45 p.m., fifteen minutes before the end of the school day, when their parents would pick them up. As soon as Felipe, Edgar, and Lance arrived to school before the end of the day, they would join their classmates in a game of baseball which they played in an atypical manner. There was no pitcher or catcher, but there was a person playing on each of the three bases with three players fanned out in the outfield. Each player hit a small red or blue rubber ball with his closed fist. Using a colored ball made it easy to strike and see as it floated through the air. Normally, Lance could wallop it very well, and he was one of the favorite players to be picked.

At 3:15 p.m. Josephine would pick Lance and Karla up at school. Acting as normal as possible, Lance would pretend all of his classes went well, so his mother would not suspect anything out of the ordinary. Chuckling to herself, Karla looked at Lance disdainfully always letting him know she was well aware of his whereabouts. At home Lance quickly changed into his shorts and basketball shoes, and off he went to the basketball court about two miles from his home. Walking through the neighborhood, Lance noticed the beautiful white walls surrounding some of the homes. Beautiful purple bougainvillea, dark red *flamboyanes* (the native blossoming trees), and other multicolored tropical flowers hung from branches over the walls and fences. On certain days, the orange and crimson rays of the sun in the late afternoon filled the sky and earth with their placating and placid hues. There was a plethora of palatial green trees and shrubs everywhere nourished by the frequent rains. Although Lance was not consciously aware of the beauty around him, he sensed the freedom and joy of being outdoors smelling the crispness of the late afternoon air. Life always seemed to run its course as naturally as the large white clouds drifting by continuously in the colossal and distant blue sky above. Lance felt a deep *raison d'être* even though it was difficult to verbalize what he was feeling.

As Lance walked through the neighborhood, thoughts about his Spanish literature class surfaced. He remembered reading *La voluntad*, a novel by José Martínez Ruiz, whose pseudonym was Azorín, a late 19th century Spanish writer. In his narrative, he describes the undulating hills, the lush green thickness of the forest, the dark light blue and turquoise hues of the ocean, the exquisite "blithe" of the white clouds, and many other resplendent landscapes of Spain's countryside. Azorín wrote about the significance of nature and its beauty as it continuously grew and mutated with each new day, leaving man with a sense of wonder and belonging. Nature had always accompanied man, and it served as a constant source of repose and solace from the tedious and frenetic pressures of civilized life. But of utmost value, Azorín viewed nature as a perpetual *corpus* of inspiration that would always permit men to find peace within themselves and with others in the world.

Lance never sensed he was alone as he walked down the sidewalk bouncing his basketball against the cement. The houses, barking dogs, gentle breeze, green shrubs, warm sunshine, and thick trees kept him company as he dribbled effortlessly. When he read *La voluntad*, he remembered Azorín's thoughts in which he admired the diverse elements of nature because they never perished. The clouds, trees, and sun have always existed, and they will continue to prevail throughout the course of time. Lance was very interested in history and ideas; at times, he wished he could control their evolution, so he could place them in a crystal ball. If this were possible, he could study them closely and unveil their hidden mysteries. Maybe he could even have a conversation with God, the ultimate source of knowledge.

BASKETBALL AND EXISTENTIALISM

When Lance arrived to the basketball court, he practiced his jump shot for thirty minutes. First, he warmed up by shooting from inside the key, at a distance of five feet from the basket; then, he worked on his shots from ten feet away. Progressively and systematically, he practiced fifteen foot shots from the outer perimeter behind the free throw line. Lance loved to hear the leather ball slide through the net, making that ubiquitous *swishing* sound heard by an infinitesimal number of players and aficionados of the game. He also reveled in jumping and feeling his body work as his legs, arms, hands, and eyes moved in unison as he released the ball.

Not only did he practice shooting, but he also worked on dribbling the ball. He would dribble diagonally across the court to an area inside its rectangular boundaries where he would pivot as he changed directions. He became ambidextrous after months and years of practicing; like every other kid, he loved to move the ball behind his back and in between his legs. Later, he worked on his layups, practicing with both his right and left hands. Being a short player, he felt it was extremely important to become adept with every aspect of the game so that he could be more effective on the court. Although he wasn't aware of it at the time, basketball taught him how to discipline himself into becoming a better player. This remarkable acumen would transfer into other areas of his life as he attended college, began to work, and married.

Throughout the seventh, eighth, and ninth grades, Lance played basketball at the club *Colegio de Ingenieros, Arquitectos y Agrimensores* (CIAA), an organization that promoted and organized basketball and baseball teams for boys of all ages. The teams from CIAA competed against each other, and they also played other organizational squads from other towns like Quebradillas, Canóvanas, Caparra, Fajardo, Manatí, Levitown, and many others outside of San Juan's greater metropolitan area. John and Josephine attended many of the basketball games, but many times, they were disappointed because Lance was snubbed from participating as much as the other boys, who were the sons of the close-knit group of parents, affiliated to the CIAA club. Furthermore, Lance was a North American and the majority of the CIAA members were Puerto Ricans; therefore, Lance and his family were always considered outsiders. The seed was planted early as Lance realized that "politics" and "favoritism" were undeniable traits of all social enclaves, not just in Puerto Rico but in every country of the world.

He leaped forward in time as he remembered later working as a Spanish and ESL teacher at the San Marcos Baptist Academy. Mr. Ramírez, who was a prominent business man owning a reputable lumber and hardware company in Texas, approached him at a teacher gathering at the beginning of the school year and indicated his surprise that he was hired by the academic institution. Their relationship prior pertained to both of them belonging to the San Marcos Runner's Club. Mr. Ramírez objected to the philosophical diatribes Lance wrote, as editor of the newsletter, in which he would relate running to maxims expressed by Plato, Socrates, Søren Kierkegaard, Friedrich Nietzsche, Karl Jaspers, and other classical thinkers. Jaspers, for example, stated that the philosopher is in constant search for God while the minister of any religious denomination has stopped seeking *son Dieu* (his God), since he already found him. Much like running, many athletes have talent, but they don't labor regularly to fine tune their ability to run faster and work through the physical, as well as the intellectual, pain required to become a better athlete and thinker.

Mr. Ramírez sent an article to be published in the newsletter relating running to Jesus Christ, which Lance happily included in the next edition. Lance was a Christian, but he was not blinded by a zealousness that, in his mind, was anti-Christian because Mr. Ramírez wanted to sideline himself from free thought. At this secondary school where his daughter attended and he was a monetary donor, Mr. Ramírez knew he could exercise his clout to subdue and squelch any oppositional views that eclipsed with his narrow-minded judgmental line of thinking. Lance knew his days were numbered due to this prejudgment, when months later, this came to fruition. The daughter shared with her father, Mr. Ramírez, the fact that one day Mr. Sullivan (Lance) mentioned the Buddha as it related to a class discussion of the different types of world faiths in her Spanish class.

After an inquisitional meeting at this private Christian school with both of the daughter's parents present in the principal's office along with Lance, he was forced to resign. This was his first "taste," so to speak, of intolerance and "terrorism" against someone like Lance who was worldly, educated, and bicultural. Lance realized he marched to the beat of a different drummer than many North Americans limited by their monolingual narrow-minded haughtiness, which limits them linguistically, intellectually, and spiritually. Lance believed Christ spoke against this type of bigotry, hypocrisy, and bombastic viewpoint, since the Lord had experienced all of this personally. The Pharisees and Jewish intellectual elite judged him on numerous occasions when he performed healings on the Sabbath and overturned the tables of merchants in God's temple. Many schooled psychologists and professional counselors today would be quick to label Christ as "bipolar" for demonstrating "controlled anger" against a political and religious establishment that rejected his claim that he was the Son of God. Jesus came to die for man's sins on the cross and resurrect on the third day to atone for the forgiveness of all people. To the influential elite of those times, Christ was a heretic who needed to be opposed and contained. Jesus Christ was basically a free thinker going against the grain of the deep-rooted establishment of those times. In Lance's mind, Mr. Ramírez was presumptuous to believe he was Jesus Christ, and Lance knew this was wrong. Mr. Ramírez was so constrained by his material success and political influence in the microcosmic town of San Marcos, Texas where he acted as if he were the Emperor Julius Caesar of this small community.

Obviously, this was Lance's opinion, one he has the freedom to espouse as an American in the United States. Globally, today, in the 21st century, this attitude demonstrated by the multitude of "Ramírez's" cohorts breeds intolerance and intellectual stagnation when dealing with international affairs in Syria, Iran, Iraq, Russia, and other countries. Domestically, for example, it leads to an inability to dialogue when confronting White police brutality against young African-Americans, as witnessed tragically in Ferguson, Missouri. The shooting death of Michael Brown on August 9th, 2014 was very tragic; the propagation of the senseless killings of White officers and primarily Blacks is unacceptable. Relating back, for a moment, to Ramírez's reaction to Buddha and his teachings, which is practiced in many Asian countries like Japan, Vietnam, Tibet, and others, one can clearly see how he formulated a judgment of those nations and people. According to him, the mentioning of the Buddha is not related to a Spanish class; however, Mr. Ramírez did not know that Miguel de Unamuno along with Miguel de Cervantes, two renown Spanish writers among a multitude of others, were inclusive of Asian cultures in their works. If you separate Buddha, for example, from schools, even Christian schools, you are severing the Christian community from others; thus, this fatal mistake breeds hatred and biases towards those who are different. Neither Christ nor Buddha wanted people to hate and despise one another. If anything, they had much in common and preached the same principles: inner and world peace, happiness, and tolerance of all people and races. Mother Teresa espoused this compassion and love as she dedicated her life to caring for the Untouchables from India. In other words, Lance was a firm believer in actions speaking louder than words. Metaphorically, Mother Teresa, being a representative of the Catholic Church, loved all people, especially, the Hindus, and she allowed Christ to work through her in an effort to assist the needy and eliminate the "terrorism" that dwells in man's broken nature, a state we all experience as humans.

Because of a lack of playing time, Lance did not consider himself to be a very good player. He still continued to practice all the time; however, he did not feel like he was making much progress. If it were not for the continual support from John, Lance probably would have quit playing basketball altogether. Lance often remembered the numerous conversations he had with his father.

Lance would often tell his father: "Dad, I feel like I should quit the team. I'm just not as good as Bituso, Ricky, Efraín, and Mamacho. Why don't I play as much as they do?"

John would always take a deep breath as he encouraged him. "Son, you are a tremendous basketball player. You dribble well, you have an excellent jump shot, and your passes are excellent. But, you have to learn there are certain things, such as politics, that neither you nor I can control. You just have to be determined to accept these obstacles and try to overcome them." Although Lance could not fully understand what John was saying, he was beginning to realize that life was not always fair.

John would often mull over his past experiences as he tried to relate them to Lance's realities. He knew it would be challenging to bring and raise his children in a foreign country, but he did not dither for a moment when he decided to move to Puerto Rico. John overcame his past qualms, good and bad, to stoke his desire to learn with an insatiable curiosity compelling him to read incessantly. He recalled reading *Self-Reliance* by Ralph Waldo Emerson, one of John's favorite writers. In this essay, Emerson develops the idea of man's need to rely and depend on himself. Society with its institutions, government, and people are good, but a person can acquiesce to the unrelenting demands of these institutions. Inherently, these big "machines" can steal a person's soul if one is not protective of his identity within the collectiveness of society. Many times people cannot separate the self from the group; thus, they drown themselves in the group's turbulent waters.

John also admired Emerson because he conveyed his views and was not afraid to think for himself. Emerson believed a man's will was a very important aspect of his life. He affirms that a child begins to apprehend the lesson of the "will" at an early age. The child chooses to play because he wants and chooses to do so. If the desire to play did not exist, the child wouldn't have indulged himself in this activity. Moreover, all of the choices man makes are kindled by his volition, and this concept aligns itself with Arthur Schopenhauer's argument of the will being the stimulus for all things in the universe. Inorganic and organic matter, in essence, result from this type of determined universe orchestrated by God for man.

On the contrary, water, for example, has a blind *will* subject to the climatically varied conditions encompassing it. Water freezes or vaporizes, and it can remain stagnant in a pond while, in another instance, it trickles into a vibrant stream from a mountain top. Water as organic matter is "visionless," since it is not conscious of its inorganic will like man is. When man chooses to build a house, for example, he is conscious of his resolve to do so. Philosophy and thought are the foundations of one's actions, and this is why John wanted his son to appreciate life as he acknowledged it through the awareness of his mind.

By exposing Lance to sports and the *political favoritism* of the CIAA Club, John knew Lance would learn a great lesson. It was one he would be able to relate and apply to the events he would encounter the rest of his life. This insight would prompt Lance to be mindful of his love and courageous decision to play basketball. Although there would be many obstacles placed in front of him, he would be better prepared to work through them successfully, maintaining his peace of mind and resolve to persevere.

John often had serious conversations with Lance, and John enjoyed seeing his son think independently. The ability to develop one's own thoughts was extremely important to John. If a person ignored his beliefs, he believed a person subjected himself to the ideas and beliefs of others; thus, he would accept these convictions without further contemplation. Because of John's strong beliefs based primarily on religion (man's faith in God) and philosophy, which compelled John to pursue his spiritual life, he firmly tried to exercise his faith on a daily basis. John procured many of his thoughts, regarding his inner being, from the readings of José Ortega y Gasset, a 20th century Spanish writer.

Ortega y Gasset expressed his philosophy with the Spanish word *"ensimismamiento,"* which means the ability to search within one's own soul to find the true meaning of life. If man did not separate himself from his external world, he would not be able to learn about himself. From time to time, it was indispensable to escape from friends, family, and society in an attempt to be alone so as to learn to understand one's own self. If a man ignores his inner self, he ignores life; therefore, it is essential to explore the hidden "morass" of the unknown world, which dwells within each individual.

One evening after dinner, Lance asked John some very profound questions which fascinated John. Lance asked, "How do you know God exists?"

"Son, this is not an easy question to answer."

"Well, in my opinion, God does not exist because I can't see him nor can I touch or speak to him, like you and I are doing right now."

John pondered and thought about Lance's argument before he replied. The famous quote, "I think therefore I am," coined by Descartes, the 17th century French philosopher, came to mind. Descartes would probably agree with Lance because if Descartes' statement were true, then it would also be correct to suggest, "I think therefore God does not exist." John continued to envisage by specifying: "Son, I feel it is fundamental to have faith in God. Man can only see and understand God by exercising his faith. Faith does not conform to the senses of touch, smell, sight, sound, or taste."

As John was thinking and discussing this topic with Lance, he remembered Aristotle's discourse on the senses and the real world. Aristotle espoused the idea that in the real world form and matter can't be experienced separately because they are one. For example, a seed represents *form* because it has a certain shape. Eventually, this seed will germinate if it is placed in fertile soil, watered, and receives plenty of sun. It will blossom into a flower or plant, which represents matter; therefore, man can see the seed grow into a flower. However, God is the Creator of this real world composed of form and matter, and He exists outside and inside of this world since He is omnipresent. The seed and the flower are elements of his creation, and God expresses himself through these components.

Lance was totally befuddled by his father's discourse. Faith was such an impalpable and abstract concept, which did not make any sense to Lance. "But Dad, how does a person acquire faith? Why does God make it so difficult for man to have faith to believe and obey his laws?"

John thought about Baruch Spinoza, a radical 17th century Dutch philosopher born to Jewish-Portuguese parents, who believed that everything in the universe (stars, animals, trees, rocks, etc.) is God. Each substance has a body and a mind. In this book *Ethics*, Spinoza relates geometry and its theories to developing his propositions. He incorporates the Latin terms *natura naturans* (nature naturing) and *natura naturata* (nature natured). Nature is equivalent to God, and he is not the Creator who exists apart from his creation as many viewed in the 17th century, but according to Spinoza's post-Cartesian views, each mode or form of life in nature is a modification or alteration of nothing other than the Divine, which is *Dieu* (God).

Furthermore, a mind cannot exist without a body, and a body cannot exist without a mind. A star, for instance, is an extension of God's universe. It is a mechanism that exists independently of mind, but when man contemplates a star, he adopts His mind. It now becomes an extension of mind; therefore, the mind and body are extensions of God who is the universe according to Spinoza, a thinker who was excommunicated from his Jewish community for his radical postulations.

John was amazed by his son's inquisitiveness and his desire to try to understand complex subjects. He knew Lance would become a good thinker because he did not accept ideas and beliefs without reflecting on their logic and truth. John encouraged him to continue meditating on his own by affirming:

You must remember your father does not know all the answers. I am just as human as you or any other person. I make many mistakes, but I do value my opinion just as I value yours. You must never assume your opinion is totally correct because we as humans are imperfect. Always remember to listen to other people's assertions and learn to respect them. Many times differences arise between people because they think their beliefs and viewpoints are correct whereas those of others are not.

God understands these rifts which exist among all men. Furthermore, I believe He chooses to test man, and this is why He allows man to make his own decisions. Moreover, God wants man to think for himself because He wants man to live and obey Him freely. All men have the ability to obey God; however, many prefer not to do so. However, I do believe it is paramount for men to try to live according to God's will so that ultimately the human race can be reunited with God in the life after death. To follow God's will, it is essential for men to communicate effectively with one another by respecting each other's differences and allowing God to influence their lives.

Lance would always cherish and value the conversations he had with his father.

Not only did Lance spend time with his Puerto Rican friends at school during the eighth grade, but he also hung out with his North American friends who lived at El Monte Apartment Complex. Lance's best friends were Raffy, Wyatt (nickname Bulldozer), and Keif. Raffy and his brother Mordechai were Puerto Ricans, but they were raised in North American families. Their mother was born in Puerto Rico, but she was raised in New York; their father was from Boston. Kelvin was a North American who had lived most of his life in the United States. Ralph was a music aficionado playing the bass guitar, and Lance cherished the fortuitous and countless hours he squandered with his friends listening to the Beatles, Jimmy Hendrix, Deep Purple, Jethro Tull, Emerson Lake and Palmer, and other popular groups during the 1970s.

Ralph also played the bass guitar in a band with another friend Carlos, who played the lead guitar. It was a time devoid of responsibilities and cares as Lance reminisced about the times he and his friends listened to vinyl records on a stereo in Carlos's room. The peace and "wildflower" paraphernalia (beads, necklaces, pins, and incense) worn by Lance and his friends where symbolic of the times, a period in which the young generation protested the war in Vietnam; they visualized a world of peace (la paix dans le monde), John Lennon style. Lance also remembered the plethora of posters: Jimi Hendrix, Henry Fonda on a motorcycle flipping off the world, Chicago and Carnegie Hall, Joni Mitchell, Three Dog Night, Pink Floyd, and others on the walls of his room; at night, he would turn on his iridescent black light and lose himself in the ecstatic *drunkenness* of his music. During the day, Lance and his friends would hang out under a shade tree and listen to Ralph and Carlos play their instruments and sing popular songs. The lyrics "We all live in a yellow submarine," and the melodies of "Purple Haze," "Imagine," or "Stairway to Heaven" along with an abundance of other tunes resonated in his mind as he tried to relive those moments through his thoughts now some forty years later.

John cherished his childhood as he observed Karla and Lance growing up. He recalled the afternoons he meandered swimming in the Rio Grande River down in the valley in Mercedes, Texas. He thought about the watermelons he and his best friend Zane used to sell on a truck as they travelled from town to town. When there were no watermelons to sell, they sold bibles. His father was a devout Christian, and John also learned to love and serve God at the tender age of seventeen.

As John reflected upon his childhood and as he observed Lance's adolescent years, he remembered Jean Paul Sartre's novel *Nausea*. In the novel, which takes the form of a diary, Sartre describes the ordinary activities of everyday life. He uses words to paint the exact picture of his room where there is an upright chair, a mahogany desk, an oxidized lamp, and an old print of Marcel Duchamp's *Nude Descending a Staircase* encased in a broken and incongruous picture frame. He also wrote about his love affairs. He would make love to a particular woman, but her name was not important to him. Neither was he concerned about sharing any feelings or sentiments with her. When he went outside, Sartre observed a leaf falling from a limb of a tree. At this point, he asks the question: "What is reality and what is fantasy?" The leaves, as well as the upright chair in his room, are objects people see daily, which is unequivocal, but few people wonder about their significance and the effect they have on their lives. The chair, for instance, is part of reality because a person would sit in it. It provided comfort; thus, it became a necessary part of his reality. When Sartre spent a night with a woman, they both were satisfying a desire. The chair, the desire, and other objects existed on their own terms. Because of their palpable *existence*, Sartre felt as if he were lost in a state of *nausea*, not knowing what was real or surreal. It's possible he felt a certain aversion towards the reality of things because they just existed without being contemplated. He could not dialogue with a lamp or a picture frame; however, most people cannot remain quiet with their thoughts long enough to truly see and perceive objects in their circumference. On the contrary, he could talk to the women he slept with choosing to treat them as objects. If he did decide to talk to them, how would he know that words and feelings were real and not surreal? Sartre was questioning man's definition of existence and reality in his novel, and this was intrinsic for him as a philosopher and writer who wanted to entice his reader to ponder *deeper waters* of thought (d'être plongé dans ses pensées).

These ruminations slipped through John's mind as he *digressed* back into the timeline of his life and compared it to Lance's experiences. Sartre's novel coerced John to reflect upon the relationship between the past and present as he responded to this pensive inclination. John scrutinized the material items, which formed a part of Lance's life, such as the black light and posters, with the watermelons, bibles, and other items, which comprised elements in his life. For some reason, John could directly relate to Sartre's depiction of objects, experiences, and feelings as all being interwoven in such a way as to create a certain nausea, or "nebulous" state of confusion, mysteriously connecting one's memories and background. Looking at existence through the pensive lenses of dissimilar writers and thinkers afforded him with the individual assessment of his life realizing that all people internalize to formulate their own answers to their personal meaning or *raison d'être*. John took much delight thinking about *la vie* (life) as he watched Lance and Karla grow up.

One day Lance and his friends were hanging out outdoors at El Monte Apartments. Lance became involved in an altercation with Kelvin, who was normally a nonaggressive kid, and Mordechai encouraged Kelvin to stand up to Lance. After being pushed by Lance, Kelvin shoved him back. Utterly behooved by Kelvin's willingness to fight back, Lance hesitated momentarily. They began to slug each other; suddenly, Kelvin pinned Lance to the ground and punched him in the nose and mouth, which caused Lance to bleed profusely.

John was watching the fight from the balcony of his apartment; as he monitored them, he emboldened Lance to do his best, knowing this was a rite of passage for both boys. John yelled out for both boys to fight fairly; somehow, Lance, encouraged by his father's words, was able to get out from underneath of Kelvin. Once he was on his feet again, he chased Kelvin in the open area sparsely landscaped with palm trees and verdant green grass refreshed by rain the night before. Kelvin felt a chill run through his body because he sensed that Lance was not going to give up. Lance burst into tears as he became more infuriated with a new surge of adrenaline. As soon as Kelvin tired of running, Lance began to punch him repeatedly until Kelvin started to cry. Kelvin said, "O.K., I don't want to fight anymore. Stop hitting me." Lance was the most relieved by his foe's acquiescence to quit. Knowing that John witnessed the fight, he felt a great sense of satisfaction creating a stronger bond between father and son. Lance admired the fact that his father really didn't take sides, but realized boys needed to fight from time to time because this was part of growing up. Obviously, he would have interfered if they were really harming each other.

John was very proud of Lance for not quitting. Lance did not totally understand this lesson at the time, but later on in life, he would remember its meaning forever. When Lance walked into his apartment, John patted him on the back and congratulated him for his courage and willingness to stand up to Kelvin. About fifteen minutes later, the doorbell rang, and to John's astonishment, Kelvin had returned with Mordechai. Kelvin retorted emphatically, "I'm ready to pick up where we left off. I was a little hungry, but now, I've eaten and want to resume fighting." John believed it was an appropriate time to intervene. "I think you guys have had enough. You both stood up to each other, and I know that you will respect one another from now on." John knew that in time both Lance and Kelvin would look back at this altercation and laugh about it. Even though Lance knew, from a boy's perspective, he had won the fight; he also realized he would never pick on Kelvin again.

In the ninth grade, Lance met Rex and Stevie. Alex was a senior who had grown up in New York with his brother Rafo. Steve was from St. Louis, Missouri, and he had just moved to Puerto Rico. Alex became Lance's best friend walking to and from school together each day. After school they regularly hung out together for a couple of hours before Lance would have to return home for dinner. Alex was like a big brother. It was special for Lance to have Alex as a friend, since he was older and enjoyed being around Lance. During the lunch hour at school, Alex, Steve, and Lance would meet under a shade tree across the street from their classrooms. They would buy a hot dog with all the garnishes from a street vendor and sit in the cool breeze talking, eating, and smoking cigarettes. This was a magical time for Lance, since he was less contumacious. It was fun to belong to a group, and this was his tribe.

At this time Lance began to experiment with marijuana. Gilberto, another one of Lance's friends, from El Monte, the large white semicircular dome shaped apartment complex where Lance lived, talked Lance into smoking pot.

"Oye, vamos a fumar un motito". (Let's go smoke a joint.) Lance responded, "Hombre, no sé si es una buena idea". (I don't think it's such a great idea.) "Te va a gustar. Te lo prometo". (You're going to like it. I promise you.) Gustavín really wanted him to get stoned. Lance was a little apprehensive, but nevertheless, he wanted to try it. He did not get high the first time he smoked, yet all he remembered was the burning sensation caused by the smoke as it filtered down his throat and lungs. He coughed and gasped for air simultaneously. Gustavín yearned to see the effect pot would have on Lance as he imagined it would be humorous to watch Lance get stultified.

Aimlessly, Lance continued to smoke pot with Gustavín, Alex, and Steve throughout the remainder of the ninth grade. Eventually, Lance would get high, which caused him to laugh uncontrollably because everything seemed so funny and blown out of proportion. It was common for Lance to get stoned with Alex in the lobby at El

Monte where fifteen to twenty kids would gather every night. In this relaxed and altered state of mind, Lance perceived everyone walking and talking in slow motion, and people's facial expressions and gestures were exaggerated. As he reflected nostalgically, he acknowledged it was a period of experimentation and of youthful play growing up in the *Woodstock Era* with Janis Joplin, Eric Clapton, Carol King, and a multitude of other rock-and-roll icons that permeated the late 1970s.

He would often reminisce about the numerous and countless hours reveling with his friends in the lobby. Subconsciously, he and his buddies relished the comfort of belonging to a close-knit clan as Ayn Rand, a Russian writer and philosopher who immigrated to the United States after leaving the oppression of communism behind, suggested in many of her novels, especially, *The Fountainhead*. Although she underscores the value of individualism and self-responsibility as embraced and portrayed in the main character Howard Roark, the successful architect of this work, Rand realizes that his success could only be possible in a capitalistic society where Americans represent a "close-knit clan" allowing for this type of individual self-realization or objectivism. For Lance, Rand's rugged proposal for self-realization and interest for others was liberating, one he would foster subliminally later in his adult life.

The guys and girls shared their feelings with one another in the lobby of the idyllic El Monte Apartment Complex in Hato Rey, Puerto Rico. They talked about their parents, dreams, interests, and desires. Lance often recalled the intimacy he felt towards Lolita. Their first kiss was archived away in the recesses of his mind forever. Lisa had dark brown hair and eyes, and the curvatures of her body were perfectly shaped. He would never forget the emptiness and ecstatic fulfillment he felt simultaneously when his lips touched hers for the first time as if savoring the nectar of uninhibited love. The soft sensation of his tongue touching hers and the smoothness of her lips resting gently upon his were two indelible memories of his adolescence. The euphoria and rapture of "puppy love" was very intense. He could never erase those sad but enticing brown eyes looking into his.

One illustrious afternoon after school, Tito and Lance climbed up the stairs leading to the rooftop of one of the two curved dome-shaped structures comprising the expansive apartment complex, which had twelve floors, the top one being the penthouse. There was an open hatch in the escape stairwell, which also housed the large incinerators on the bottom basements. Each floor had an opening for dispensing of rubbish to flow down to be set ablaze in the large dispensers. It was a very cloudy day, and there was a slight breeze blowing the nebulous cotton swabs above supported by invisible threads from the heavens. Lance was afraid to look over the edge since he was acrophobic just like his father. As they sat on the roof, Rafo pulled out a joint consisting of a Colombian cut of marijuana, one considered *primo* back in the day, and enthusiastically articulated: "Let's get ripped, dude!" (¡Vamos a arrebatarnos, bro!) Lance was excited, "Yeah. I hope this is some good shit, since I really feel like getting high."

It wasn't long before the clouds snowballed around Lance's face and eyes. He was instantly flushed with the sensation of floating haphazardly in the sky, and he couldn't feel the force of gravity pulling him down. He lost his sense of balance as he imagined himself thrown into space. Some indescribable force pulled him towards a distant star. Its brightness blinded him as he somersaulted through the weightless air. Slowly, his eyesight adjusted to the erratic movement of passing comets and humongous galaxies. He saw a one-eyed cat floating by chasing a polychromatic mouse carrying an umbrella. It was wild! Every time the cat got close to the mouse it fell ten feet, and then it would regain its balance again. The mouse floated by mocking the cat by pointing his enlarged finger at him and laughing uncontrollably. This perceived existentialist innocuous state of mind or *flow of consciousness* embraced by many literary writers such as, the French Jean-Paul Sartre, the Mexican Augustín Yáñez, and the Colombian Gabriel García Márquez with his *magical realism* along many other acclaimed authors would entice Lance. Later in life, he remembered this specific *altered state of being* of his youth as a movie he could replay in his mind. Lance could not recall the conversation he had with Rafo that afternoon because everything seemed so equivocal; however, it was a surreal smoke with some *psychedelic hyperbole* he added to it later. All Lance commemorated was the one-eyed cat chasing the mouse in vain lost in the rhapsody of the popular lyrics of Carly Simon: "You're so vain. I bet you think this song is about you." It was a mesh of imaginary thoughts and visions embellished later as he wrote this novella. He also recollected going home and right to bed. Josephine was stunned, since Lance seemed so tired so early in the day never suspecting her son was stoned.

Lance would cherish this experience and compare it to those of Augusto Pérez, the main character in the novel *Niebla* by Miguel de Unamuno, the Spanish writer of the 19th-20th centuries. Augusto remained in a confused state or nebula when he had several conversations with God after his fiancée took his money and married another man. Augusto could not understand why God allowed this to happen to an honest and good man like himself.

"God, why is this happening to me? You are a good God, and I'm a good person. I don't understand your point of view."

God responded, "Man of little faith, you must learn to trust and believe in me. You love life more than you love me. I do not exist in the realms and corridors of reason. You cannot logically understand me. You must rely on faith to begin to comprehend my greatness."

But God, "I do have faith. I pray and go to church like a good Christian. I truly love and believe in you."

"Yes, you do work hard at it. However, you're a slave to routine which is good. Going to church and praying is important, and these actions please me. Yet, you have to learn to live and breathe with your soul. You have to commune with me always, not just on Sundays."

Furthermore, God explains to Augusto that there are certain things man cannot control; consequently, man cannot blame God for all his misfortunes. Man has to learn to accept these sufferings. Augusto is totally defeated and dies at the end because he cannot overcome his grief. At the end of the novel, Augusto's dog, who is his best friend, tells God he can no longer go on existing without his master. The dog also perished from grief at the end of the novel.

Strangely enough Lance compared his life to Augusto's because he often questioned his existence. Lance could not comprehend what was happening to him spiritually, mentally, and philosophically. He was living in a foreign culture, which also compounded the problem, as well as being torn between his parents and his friends, who were both North American and Puerto Rican. Getting *"arrebatado"* (stoned) avowed him to question his background and identity. He did not consider this an escape, but a quest and search for meaning. He was conversing with God in his own way.

Lance always recalled the day when he got ripped with Rafo. Maybe God was trying to communicate something to him. God may have been asking Lance: "What are your values? What do you want from life?" Lance knew it was important to evaluate and understand his emotions and feelings. Neither his life nor anyone else's was perfect; however, it seemed clear to him that he could learn quite a bit about himself if he willfully desired to do so. Later on in life, when he read a passage by Johann Gottlieb Fichte, a German philosopher of the 18th and 19th centuries, who stressed the significance of establishing a kind of coexistence between one's consciousness and physical being, Lance began to listen and follow the intuitions of his inner soul. He made it a point to act upon his inner feelings and emotions realizing one could affect the other positively or negatively. For example, noticing the quiet beauty of a silent river while slowly floating downstream in a kayak creates a sense of well-being and happiness. Conversely, if one's view and perception of this idyllic scenery was obscured by thoughts of a faraway and unpleasant discussion earlier in the day with one's boss, the built up negativity would prompt a sense of discomfort and sadness.

Lance's freshman year was a very memorable one for him because he started smoking pot and hanging out with Alex. They were best friends, and they spent a lot of time together. Lance looked up to Alex and respected him because he was older. As Lance reminisced about his adolescent years in Puerto Rico, it was easy for him to envision Alex walking in the distance: wearing a pair of faded Lee jeans, a blue tee shirt with a side pocket, and a pair of dingo boots smoking a Marlboro cigarette. They shared many dreams together. They often talked about running away to New York to find a job and meet some ravishing chicks. They enjoyed talking about girls, and Alex often teased Lance, since he had never gone all the way with a girl before. He often chuckled and said: "Man one of these days you'll know what it's like to get your stick wet. Ha, ha! You're just a chump, man. When we get to New York, we'll meet some cool babes. The women there know what they want. They're not as wishy-washy like the Puerto Rican chicks."

At the time Lance did not realize the importance of dreams. Without them man could neither envision the future nor could he understand the past or present. Dreams keep people alive, since they are the backdrop for people's goals. They represent the intangible dichotomy between reality and fantasy, one stressed by Miguel de Cervantes in his infamous novel *Don Quijote de la Mancha*. Man cannot understand his reality if he does not lose himself in the world of fantasy. When man searches and explores his fantastic world, he realizes who he is and finds his meaning for being. In the dream state, he dwells in the subconscious or the collective unconscious world, one defined by Carl Jung, the well-known 20th century Swiss psychologist, in his book *Man and His Symbols*.

Lance would soon discover how society slowly molds men to believe that fantasy is not relevant to the issues of the modern world. Society and its institutions teach men to conform and be practical, especially, in the United States. Being pragmatic means getting an education and a job that pays well so that man can support himself and his family. Getting the best possible education means going to the best schools such as Harvard, Yale, Oxford, and other coveted universities.

Unfortunately, obtaining an elite education has become a status symbol. Many educators have lost the ability to teach because their capricious ways and insatiable desire to be successful have driven them down the wrong path. Education is no longer an ideal where people share commensurate ideas with one another. It has become a stagnant whirlpool in which intellectuals pretend to be erudite. Society has created academic buffoons who spend more time researching than teaching; thus, students have to learn on their own as many professors go about their business preserving their pseudo-Darwinism in the wake of their own ignorance. Universities fail to educate because money and prestige go to those fickle educators, for the most part, who publish and who rarely spend time in the classrooms teaching. And when the professor does teach, he lectures to his students, who do not learn how to think for themselves, because they are deprived of engaging in a meaningful dialogue.

This method of teaching allows the professor to feed his ego as he pontificates. Free thought and thinking are not encouraged; therefore, many students fulfill their requirements and graduate from college and lead practical and complacent lifestyles. The ability to think and question life and the issues of the world are skills they never acquired. Education becomes the means to an end as it might lead to a well-paying job for some, but it doesn't, in the majority of cases, foster a cultured individual. The prestige and money guide many to a *neurotic narcissism* defined by the Mercedes they drive, the multimillion dollar home where they live, and the Gucci shoes they wear without an original thought of their own.

Intrinsically drawn to the realm of ideas and philosophical ruminations, Lance felt a constant yearning inside, which motivated him with an unquenchable desire to learn about himself and the world around him. He would often remember with nostalgia his silhouette frolicking on the sidewalk or grass as he walked pensively to school in the early light of dawn. The redness of the flamboyán flowers and the sweet smells of roses encroached upon his thoughts as he walked through the mysterious labyrinth of each day. Everything seemed so vibrant, alive, and full of color and vigor. The freshness of the morning dew, the innocent songs of sparrows and titmice birds, and the golden teardrops of the sun danced on the damp *vereda* (path) in front of him. His thoughts and the beauty around him would always keep him company. Often he preferred the company of these impressions rather than the chatter and noise created by people.

Later in life Lance would read and learn more about the significance and insignificance of man in the world through the words of Henry David Thoreau, the 19th century American poet and writer, who influenced his thoughts and beliefs when ascertaining: "I love the birds and beasts because they are myth logically in earnest. I see that the sparrow cheeps and flits and sings adequately to the great design of the universe; that man does not communicate with it, understand its language, because he is not one with nature." These words impregnated Lance's thoughts as he assimilated the value of viewing the kaleidoscopic hues of early sunrises, the soothing tumultuous sounds of waves gently resting on the sand, and the awesome view of colossal mountains hidden in the billows of the horizon. Man could learn to understand himself by contemplating nature and voluntarily immersing himself within its confines to find the solitude and peace he craves subconsciously. Without this kind of introspection, man would lose his sanity in a world controlled by the human ego and its need to suppress him and others, including the natural world that circumvents him.

Other than Alex and Steve, Lance had two other good friends who were also older than he was. Rolly and Joszef (God will Add), two brothers from Colombia, South America, lived on the sixth floor of El Monte Apartment Complex. Rawli had long curly blond hair, which covered his neck. His proportional physique and stark green eyes attracted the girls. Juanesto was tall and slender, and he also had long brown hair. He walked with a slow but steady cadence, and he was a lady's man as well. They both were very intelligent, active, and athletic. Rawli was twenty-seven years old and Juanesto was twenty-six. Rawli was studying physical education at the University of Puerto Rico, whereas Juanesto was majoring in business administration at La Universidad Interamericana in Santurce, a subdivision of San Juan's metropolitan area. Rawli was an excellent swimmer, who set several records on the Puerto Rican Swim Team, excelling in the 400-meter butterfly stroke, which was his favorite. Lance really admired and respected Rawli because he was amicable, popular, and athletic. He quickly noticed as well that all the girls were attracted to his robust physique and personality. Rawli spoke some English, and he enjoyed dating American girls who did not seem as conservative and restrictive as some of the Latin girls. Juanesto was also a good athlete even though he was not as gifted as his brother. Similarly, he preferred dating American girls as well, which did not go unnoticed by the younger Lance, who was impressed by their carefree attitude towards living.

Rawli took an interest in Lance, and he treated him as a younger brother. Rawli always disapproved of Lance smoking pot, although he smoked from time to time, because he felt Lance had some athletic talent, which should be developed. Many times Rawli and Lance would run four or five miles together. It was also exciting to play soccer with Rawli and Juanesto because they were very skillful and played well. Being athletically inclined, Rawli would also play basketball with Lance and his other friends although it wasn't his forte. Lance really respected him for his competitive spirit and positive demeanor towards sports and life.

Besides the ninth grade being a memorable year for Lance, he struggled with his mixed identity within the Puerto Rican society as he still contemplated running away. This still perplexed him as he wrestled with whether he was a Puerto Rican or a North American. At times, he repudiated his ability to speak Spanish fluently because most of his gringo friends only spoke English. He also wanted to learn more about the North American culture, and his fascination with taking off to New York was a constant reminder of just that. This captivating thought was much idealized because he loved his parents very much; for the most part, he wouldn't act on this impulse. Nevertheless, he was truly grappling with the internal turmoil he felt inside.

Miraculously, that year it just so happened that his grandparents, who lived in Columbia, Missouri, invited Karla to live and go to school there for one year. Karla was not sure whether she wanted to spend her senior year at a new high school. When their grandparents offered their home to Karla, her Aunt Julie (nickname Judee) and Uncle Derrick, who lived in Kansas City, Missouri, also extended an invitation for her to live with them for one year. Karla finally accepted her grandparents offer; Lance asked his parents if he could live for one year in Kansas City with his aunt and uncle, who both agreed to have him reside with them. John and Josephine both gratefully consented, since they realized it would be a great opportunity for both children to experience living in the United State.

At the end of the ninth grade, Lance said goodbye to Alex and his other friends. Lance told Alex he would keep in touch by letter, but unbeknownst to him, this would be the last time he would ever see Alex again. He was really going to miss Alex and his other friends, but he knew he had to take this trip to fully unveil the confusion and dual identity that bewildered him living on the island. That summer Karla and Lance lived in Columbia, Missouri with their grandparents. Their grandfather Laurence Robertson owned the Chef Cafeteria in downtown Columbia where Karla and Lance worked for two or three hours every night. Karla normally served food in the front, and Lance usually worked in the back washing dishes with Terry. Besides washing dishes, Lance would also help clear tables.

Mr. Robertson would often get angry with Lance and Terry because many times they would goof off when they were supposed to be working in the back. Frequently, they were caught laughing and telling stories embellished by numerous water fights with the dangling hose used for washing dishes. When Lance was not whimsically working at the eatery, he would walk over to the gymnasium at the University of Missouri and shoot baskets. He spent many afternoons playing basketball alone or with other kids who showed up to play.

Lance always dreamt about playing basketball at a big university like Missouri. As he dribbled the ball, he wondered what it would be like running a fast break against some of the greatest players in the nation. He imagined himself weaving and vacillating through defenses taking the open jump shot. He relished the sound of the crackling wood floor as he quickly changed directions zigzagging down the floor. The ball *swooshing* through the net made him feel invincible. He thought about how many other boys had these same dreams and felt this indomitable. Dreams provided a sense of wondering which was comforting and very reassuring.

After shooting baskets for several hours, Lance would run a few laps around an indoor track built around the circumference of the basketball court. Lance had never run around an indoor track like this one before, but he liked the curiosity it instilled in him as he observed his surroundings. The exterior structure that housed the interior of the gymnasium represented a Greek classical motif, which starkly contrasted with the old musty odors inside. He remembered being overwhelmed with the strength and age of this stoic building when he worked out on the basketball court. He thought about the *battles* that had been won and lost as he looked at the glassy trophy case inside on the second floor. When he walked into this modern *parthenon* for the first time, he just wanted to find the basketball court craving its solitude. He knew he was in charge, and his thoughts mixed well with the shadows of light emanating from the opposite side of the court where a distant window kept him company. Remote voices and resounding echoes of rackets and tennis balls permeated the silence of the gym. This hall of discipline and dreams preempted the direction he would take, since sports would always be a part of his life.

Every afternoon Lance would play basketball in the old gymnasium, but during the day, he went to summer school and took an algebra class at one of the local junior high schools. He did not fancy the idea of attending summer school, especially, to retake algebra because he did not have a math teacher that made the subject relevant to his life. In Puerto Rico, the year before, Lance had taken algebra; however, he did not do well because he spent most of his time playing hooky and fooling around. If it were not for John's help and his decision to confine Lance in the house for a whole weekend to prepare for a final exam in his math class, Lance would not have passed the ninth grade.

Being in Missouri again prompted Lance to think of the summer he spent with his grandparents two years earlier. That summer he took a seventh grade English class at the local junior high school. In this class Mrs. Stevenson, who was more engaging than his math teachers, had students write short stories, participate in show and tell activities, and read. During the morning break at 10 a.m., the kids were granted time to play kickball and basketball out in the schoolyard and gymnasium. Lance did not make a lot of friends in class because he was an outsider. There was a group of three boys: Brian, Jim, and Earl who were best friends and always hung out together. They often picked on Lance shoving and ridiculing him.

Lance was very sensitive, and he wanted to befriend some of the kids in class; however, he inherently knew that his upbringing and mannerisms were different. His outlook on life, after living in Puerto Rico, caused him to be a little more introverted than most students his age. He spoke Spanish fluently, and he could switch fluidly between English and Spanish. Many kids thought it was odd to be bilingual, and there was no imminent need to accommodate him in their group.

The other boys sensed Lance's divergences and seemingly independent nature; therefore, it was easy and fun to aggravate Lance. Often they would shove him in the halls, and they would not pick him to play on their team. Earl was the leader of the group who coerced the others to continually exclude him from the group's activities and games.

When Lance was older he would look back at this experience and think of Darwin's theory of evolution. Darwin's theory, which emphasized the survival of the fittest, intrigued Lance. In addition, Lance also recaptured one of the themes of the novel *Paz en guerra* by Miguel de Unamuno, the late 19th century Spanish novelist. In this work Unamuno describes the struggle of nature in the last chapter. For instance, he describes the vine that grows incessantly as it strangles the trees and plants within its reach. The vine, being the metaphor of nature's survival of the fittest, killed other forms of plant life in order to survive and live. Unamuno also observed the tall pine and oak trees that outgrew the other trees as they absorbed all the sunlight and water, which prevented the other lower forms of vegetation from maturating. The lower forms subsisted, but he detected they were subservient to their stronger masters.

When Lance was in the seventh grade, he didn't understand or know about Darwin or Unamuno; however, he did rely on instinct as he confronted this situation with *les trois amis* (three friends), which intrigued him. After experiencing a few similar situations in Puerto Rico, he cognized it was essential to isolate Earl, the leader of the group. Lance recognized from previous experiences that if he confronted him by himself, he would be able to nip the problem in the bud, so to speak. Henceforth, one afternoon Lance looked up Earl's address in the phone book and asked his grandmother to drop him off at his house, prefabricating the notion they were going to hang out for a while. At about 1:30 p.m., Grandma Patricia drove him over to Earl's place.

Patricia asked, "What are you boys going to do today? Are you going to see a movie? *The Sound of Music* is playing at the downtown theater. That is such a wonderful movie."

"I'm not sure what we will do grandma. We might play cards, and who knows, maybe we will go see a movie later. I'm sure Earl would love to see that movie. He's such a nice and peaceful boy if you know what I mean."

She dropped him off on the street in front of Earl's home. Lance waited patiently across the street, hoping Earl would walk outside. After about thirty minutes, Earl came outside with his mother, and they both got into the car.

Lance was able to see where they were going from the distance and hitched a ride from an eighteen-wheeler, which was miraculously going in the same direction, on a nearby freeway just a block away. From the truck, Lance could see where the car was turning and asked the truck driver if he would drop him off at the following exit. Lance also noticed that Earl and his mother pulled into a doctor's complex not too far away. At that moment, Lance asked the driver to stop and let him off, which he gladly conceded to do. Sweat began to trickle down Lance's forehead as he started thinking about his forthcoming confrontation with Earl. While envisioning nervously what might occur, he just wanted to leave an impression on Earl so that he would discontinue his abusive behavior towards Lance at school.

RUMINATIONS IN MISSOURI AND NEW YORK

Lance cornered Earl in the vestibule of the dentist's office, and Earl was astonished to see him. Lance said, "Well, do you feel like pushing me around now that your buddies aren't here?" Earl was speechless and totally baffled. Before Earl could move, Lance hit Earl in the face with a closed fist. Earl was so stunned that he could not defend himself, never having experienced such an overt and unconscionable reaction from anyone before in his life. What Lance had done seemed so bizarre, and he felt as if a million pound weight had been lifted off of his shoulders. After confronting Earl and taking a stand, Lance walked over to a nearby telephone booth and called his grandmother to pick him up.

From that day on, Lance did not have any more problems with Earl and his friends. For some particular reason, Earl gained some respect for Lance's courage and blatant behavior. He was so bewildered by what had happened that he did not know how to react; however, he knew he would never shove Lance around anymore.

Many years later, Lance would ponder the significance of this event which made him think about how many kids wanted and needed to be respected. Many gangs had evolved across the nation (the Mexican

Mafia, the Bloods, the Crips, and others); many kids were motivated to join a gang because of the reverence they would obtain from others. It has transcended into sports, and the deference one gained among teammates after giving one's best effort. Evidently, they were not esteemed at home because, in many instances, their parents fought or had divorced. In school, they were not treated fairly or equally because of the color of their skin, or because they were not interested in the classroom work. As a result, they had this need to be someone. Everyone wants to be recognized for who they are. It seems as if this is a value that has been lost in today's society. People get so involved with their work and leisure activities they forget about the children, who need to be nourished, loved, and appreciated.

The confrontation Lance had with Earl happened two years ago, but by going to summer school again in the same building, he became retrospective of that day. He laughed humbly as he recalled the expression on Earl's face at the doctor's office with the hope that a similar encounter like this one would not happen again. That summer he met a girl who was a few years older than he was. She had been keeping an eye on Lance all summer long; however, he was not aware of her interest in him. Being very subtle about her feelings towards him, he began to notice her friendliness as well as her long black hair and well-defined figure. She would hang around outside of his classroom during breaks; after catching her looking at him, he struck up a conversation with her one day. They both rode their bicycles to class, so they had something in common to talk about.

As the semester was ending, they spent more time chatting and getting to know one another. Lance was very coy with girls, so at first, it was very awkward and uncomfortable being around her. Her beauty dazzled him, and he never imagined himself meeting a girl in Missouri. They talked for several minutes. She asked him, "How is your algebra class coming along?"

Lance replied, "I think it's coming along alright. I barely passed algebra this past year with a D, so I often feel like a dunce in this class. What is your name, and what classes are you taking this summer?"

"I'm taking world history, and I like the class very much. I have a very enthusiastic teacher who allows us to present some creative skits in class depicting some of the major events in history. I pretended to be Cleopatra this past week. It's very stimulating and a lot of fun. By the way, my name is Debbie. What's yours?"

"My name is Lance, and I'm staying here this summer with my grandparents. My grandfather owns the Chef Cafeteria downtown. Have you eaten there?"

"No, I haven't, but maybe I'll check it out someday. Listen, I have to leave a little early today, but would you like to come over to my house tomorrow after school? We can listen to some music and hang out. We can also ride our bikes there from school. I really like your nice blue bike."

"Ummmm, yeah, that sounds like a great idea!" Lance could feel his heart pulsating tenaciously. He had never experienced titillation like this before, and he wondered if this was the innervation one felt preceding love. "I'm sure it won't be a major problem. Thanks a lot for inviting me, and I'll see you tomorrow."

The following day after school, Debbie and Lance rode their bicycles to her house. Lance was very excited because she was very attractive and older than he was. He felt a little *maladroit* (clumsy), since he did not have much experience dating. They arrived to Debbie's house around three o'clock, and both of her parents were at work. They sat down on the couch and listened to some music. They talked about school, and Lance shared some of his experiences growing up in Puerto Rico. Debbie was very attentive, and she liked Lance very much.

"How do you like Columbia, Lance?"

Debbie's eyes sparkled as she looked at Lance. She hoped he would sit a little closer to her. She sensed he was a little hesitant.

"I like Columbia a lot. I wish I could stay longer, but I have to return to Puerto Rico at the end of August."

Lance wanted to kiss Debbie, but he was very nervous. He didn't want to blow it.

Debbie slowly edged her way closer to him, but Lance was not picking up on her signals. After talking for an hour, Lance told her he had to leave. He was supposed to work at the Chef Cafeteria that afternoon. Lance felt very empty and dispirited when he stood up leaving Debbie feeling rejected. Lance really wanted to kiss her; however, he did not have enough experiences with girls to know if it was too soon to make a move. They looked at each other as Lance left and rode his bike back to town. They knew they would probably never see each other again, since they lived far away from one another. There was something magical and innocent about the time they spent together, but a cloud of melancholy hung over him. Life seemed so easy to understand at times, but at other moments, it was perplexing. Trying to comprehend and rationalize one's emotions was not an easy task.

The next day, on a Sunday afternoon, Lance was playing badminton with Karla in the capacious backyard of their grandparent's house. Adjacent to their yard was a huge field, probably about ten acres. Lance would commemorate the many afternoons he and Karla played badminton next to the field full of daises, poppies, and many other wild flowers. They gamboled freely and carelessly on a regular basis. The sun was always bright, and their smiles always gleamed as they played and palpitated with a certain freedom, an intangible ecstasy that was accompanied by the continuous motion of flowers swaying, glowing, and flitting in the wind.

As they struck the shuttlecock back and forth, Lance began to daydream and ruminate about the afternoon he spent with Debbie. He had a hard time concentrating on the game.

Karla yelled out, "When are you going to start focusing on the game?" She knew Lance was thinking about something else.

"Alright, now I'm going to get serious. You better watch out." Lance tried to fixate more on the game but continued to think about Debbie: her sleek black hair, dark green eyes, and the soft contours of her body. He decided to go visit her on his bike later that afternoon. It took him about an hour to get to her house. He was really nervous because he knew her parents would probably be home. He knocked on her door, and Debbie opened it. He could sense her uneasiness, since she didn't have the same sparkle in her eyes. Lance was extremely apprehensive as he searched for the right words. "I forgot to tell you something the other day." She said, "What?" He edged close to her and kissed her on the lips. Debbie allowed his lips to touch hers, but she pulled away. She felt a little distraught and confused after the other afternoon.

"Well, Lance, I have to go. My parents are home."

"I understand. I wish things would have turned out differently." "So do I Lance. Bye! You're a very sweet guy."

They would never see each other again. Life at its different stages seemed so strange at times. Lance would think about this encounter some twenty years later, and the expression "amor vincit omnia" came to mind. "Love conquers all." At that time, it sure didn't seem like love conquered the relationship which never developed between Debbie and Lance. Maybe, a more appropriate saying would be: "Fear conquers everything." Fear of the unknown and fear of tomorrow remain with us when love is not present. Lance knew it was impossible to predict the outcome of relationships and the future, especially, during adolescence. He wished he could anticipate his actions, feelings, and the events of his life from one day to the next. If this were possible, he knew there would probably be no need for philosophy, and more importantly, for God. Lance remembered the words of Francis Bacon, an English philosopher from the 16th-17th centuries, who stated: "Men had withdrawn themselves from contemplation of nature and the observation of experience, and they have tumbled up and down in their own reason and conceits." More importantly, Lance knew he had to rely more on faith and contemplation rather than reason. Reasoning oftentimes left a person befuddled, whereas quiet contemplation filled the heart and mind with peace.

Lance continued musing about life and its uncertainties. He believed if man lived in a perfect world, maybe he could predict the outcomes of the future. However, man is oftentimes misled by his rational thoughts and behaviors. He becomes confused when he depends too much on logical assessments. His emotions are like the wind, which blows in different directions for no reasonable explanation. Therefore, man must contemplate life and its circumstances as he searches to understand his condition. Lance knew it was essential for man to let go of his rational and analytic consciousness periodically to understand his inner self. To comprehend the irrational world of emotions, he must let go of his compulsion to rationalize. Love cannot be categorized logically, but people will probably continue to die of heartaches as they constantly try to control and dominate their sentiments. If man could ever listen to God and nature and acquiesce more readily to life's impulses, things would evolve in their own time, which would make it easier to comprehend the nuances of living.

The summer had come and gone, and now Lance was playing blackjack with some friends during study hall at Grandview High School in Kansas City, Missouri. It had been two years, since he returned to Missouri; he was spending one year with his aunt and uncle in Kansas City. It was his sophomore year in high school. He chose to come to Missouri, since he was getting into a lot of trouble in Puerto Rico selling drugs and stealing records, clothes, and other items from department stores. Lance was going through a rebellious stage, and he was also trying to come to terms with his identity. He was North American; however, he sometimes believed he was more of a Puerto Rican. He and his best friend Alex had continued to talk about running away to New York. Alex often reminded him, "Hey man! Let's take off to New York. We'll get some good jobs and meet some real babes." Lance was always a little hesitant, but he thought it was a cool idea. "Yeah man. That sounds great!"

Anyway, now, Lance was in Kansas City. During study hall, he would often think about the experiences he had two years ago in Columbia, Missouri when he confronted Earl and met Debbie. He would never forget her, and it was a mystical sensation knowing you will probably never see someone again. There was so much he wanted to say to her, but now the experience was only a memory. Nostalgic moments were sometimes good when past situations had a definite beginning and ending; however, at times, they were incomplete when what one experienced was not fulfilled. The incompleteness of life was bewildering but entertaining for meditative purposes.

Lance enjoyed living with his Aunt Julie and Uncle Derrick. Uncle Derrick would often take him fishing and hunting for bullfrogs. It was nice to be outdoors enjoying natural settings. Lance would never forget the time they went to visit his grandparents in Columbia. Uncle Derrick and Lance walked over to a private golf course across the street at midnight in their pursuit of searching and attempting to catch some bullfrogs. There was a pond in the middle of the golf course, and they could hear the frogs croaking as they approached the water. The necessary gear for hunting them was pretty basic. All you needed was an empty pillowcase, a flashlight, and some nimble strong hands.

They circumvented the pond silently, and Uncle Derrick used the flashlight to look for the frogs resting in the thick brush of tall grass on the edges of the pond. They listened intently for the croaking baritone sounds the bullfrogs would make. Once they silently crept up on a frog, his uncle blinded it with the light emanating from his flashlight; Lance sneaked up behind it slowly and very stealthily. Lance carefully dropped down on his knees and swiftly grabbed the frog with his right hand. He had to grasp it firmly because it was very slippery. Then, Lance would place it in the pillowcase. At first, the frog would jump around, but after a few minutes, it would remain quiet and very still.

Years later, when Lance was sitting at his home, a small bungalow built in the 1930s, in San Marcos, Texas where he was writing one of his many novels, he would vividly remember this particular time when he hunted bullfrogs with his uncle. He thought about the lectures of Ralph Waldo Emerson, which he had read just recently. Emerson described the eye as being the "instrument" which facilitated man's interpretation of his surroundings. Without the eye man could not see the beauty around him; therefore, without it he could not internalize and bring nature into his being. The whole meaning of life was interpreted by the eye if one knew how to "look" and see things in their true essence.

Furthermore, José Ortega y Gasset describes the importance of looking and seeing in his book *Meditations on Hunting*. He compares the hunter to the philosopher who observes nature and the circumstances of life. Ortega y Gasset states: "Like the hunter in the absolute 'outside' of the countryside, the philosopher is the alert man in the absolute 'inside' of ideas, which are also an unconquerable and dangerous jungle."

Lance admired Emerson and Ortega y Gasset because they understood life, and they "respected" and admired its true value to man. His fascination with ideas, philosophy, and history led him to many intellectual divagations. He often looked back at history as he thought about how God created the world, the oceans, and skies in five days. Then, he created man from the dust of the earth along with the flora and fauna to satisfy man's needs in life. Not only was nature meant to inspire man with its beauty; however, it was also intended to provide the food and air necessary for his survival. God also created women so that man and woman could love each other and keep one other company. In addition, it is very interesting to note that man was formed from dust; when he dies, his body decomposes and returns to the elements of the earth. Therefore, birth, life, and death complete a full circle, which recurs continuously.

These pleasant memories of the past would always accompany Lance, whether he was in the classroom, on the basketball court, or at his grandfather's cafeteria. During the last two weeks of the summer of 1974, Lance's parents afforded Lance the opportunity to attend a basketball camp in Monticello, New York. It was a well-known camp, and Walt Frazier, the current professional guard for the New York Knicks, would be appearing on several occasions. Lance was very excited, since he loved the game. He would often watch the professional basketball games on T.V. every Sunday afternoon when he was younger. Now, he had the fortuitous privilege to see some great players, like Walt Frazier, Charlie Scott, and others, play right in front of him while he watched from the sideline.

One Sunday afternoon, during the first week of August 1974, Mr. and Mrs. Robertson drove Lance to the Saint Louis, Missouri Airport where he would catch a flight to the JFK International Airport in New York City. It was always difficult to leave people you loved even when it was just for a couple of weeks. Lance was very taciturn the whole way with an aura of melancholy stirring within. Mr. Ware, John's old college buddy, met Lance at the JFK Airport and helped him make his connecting flight to Monticello, New York. Once in New York, they shared lunch together; afterwards, he transported Lance to another airport where he boarded a twin-engine plane to Monticello. This flight was very scary because the plane dipped and dived intermittently. Lance had never been on an airplane this small, and he never overcame the queasy sensation until the plane finally landed. He quiescently mumbled to himself, "Eureka, Eureka."

The landing was very anticlimactic because he was sure he would perish into oblivion from the impact. When the plane came to a halt and the engines were shut off, Lance deplaned immediately. A rather corpulent woman wearing a floral dress was having trouble exiting the plane. Lance had a phobia he would not be able to get off. He certainly did not want to fly back to JFK.

Once inside the Monticello Airport, Lance located a taxi, which transported him to the downtown bus station where he called Mr.

Jones, the man from the Kutsher's Sports Academy who was going to pick him up. The taxi driver dropped him off at a sketchy bus station leaving him a little apprehensive because it was a busy and frenetic city with people and bustling cars going in every direction. Lance walked into the station and called Mr. Jones from a public telephone booth. After dialing, he began to speak.

"Hello! May I speak to Mr. Jones?"

"Yes, this is he. Whom am I speaking with?"

"This is Lance Sullivan, and I have just arrived to Monticello. I'm waiting at the bus station."

"We're a little backed up, but I'll be sending Mr. Allen Brown down to pick you up. It might take a while, maybe 30 to 40 minutes."

"That's fine. I'll be waiting in front of the bus station. I have a green duffle bag."

"We'll see you soon. Welcome to Monticello."

Outside the bus station, a morose ambience filled the surroundings as Lance sat down on his duffle bag and watched the implacable streets full of moving cars and buses. A plethora of young and old people ambulated up and down the narrow sidewalks. He felt as if he were riding on one giant Ferris wheel, and the circular mechanism kept revolving over and over again as he continued to see glimpses of scenery composed of people, streets, and vehicles. He looked down one street alley, and there seemed to be no end. The road led to some unknown corridor or hall in his mind. Lance repainted the vividness of the red-bricked walls, which bordered the street with large aluminum trash cans spread out along the alley. It had a determined symmetry of its own. Smoke billowing spiraled upwards towards the sky in the back of the alley, emanating from what appeared to be a heater vent. A dark black and grey dog trotted precariously, looking, and internalizing. The dog seemed insensitive and immune to the stark and loud nuances of the city. It did not care as it mechanically meandered to the back of the street, the only place it could hide and find solace.

A man noticed Lance sitting on this duffle bag outside the bus station. The man wore a bright floral shirt and dark pants, and his obese body swayed from left to right as he walked down the sidewalk. He approached Lance who was nervously watching the busy streets and looked vulnerable and disconcerted. The man sensed Lance's uneasiness as he converged closer to him. When he walked past Lance, he flashed a twenty-dollar bill in front of him. This did not surprise Lance because in Puerto Rico he had encountered many situations in which a homosexual or some sort of pervert approached him; as a result, he ignored the man's overtures. It was obvious he wanted to lure Lance into accepting the money in exchange for some sort of sexual favor. Lance could not fully understand why there were so many deviant malcontents in today's society.

Inadvertently, Lance decided to wait for his ride inside the bus station. Luckily, the malicious man did not follow him as he found a seat by the window and resumed gazing out into the crowd. The cluster of people outside amazed him, all wandering in different directions and living multifarious realities. His meandering thoughts took him to a beach far away in the Caribbean where the wind blew constantly and gently. The water was of a turquoise hue, and the sand was white and soft. The intensely luminous sun was brilliantly bright in the background as the piercing rays espoused the transparent water and breeze of the early dawn. The morning dew rested its head upon the tumbling waves as they gained force, crashing against the shore. The sound of the sea pounding against the packed sand effervesced instilling within him a complete sense of happiness. Inexplicably, at that moment, he was led to think of Lord Byron's poetry. The rhythm of the sand and sea lifted his soul. The soul being the indomitable force which men could not ignore because it was the life source of existence. Lord Byron, the English poet of the 19th century, had written a love poem "Parsimonia," which really moved Lance. In the poem, Byron describes the brown hue of a leaf falling from a tree in the midst of winter. He also described the sublime beauty of the ubiquitous sunrise refreshing and renewing the soul with its soothing touch of crimson and orange palpitations.

Byron also depicts the early morning dew watering each blade of grass in that fine hour right before the rising sun. The poet was able to transcend to a place where the soul of each man would attempt to go, but somehow fails to arrive. He sees life and observes its minute details that enrich and elevate us to an understanding and appreciation, which transcend the chaos and confusion of everyday living. Byron uses these metaphors to elevate the significance of love and relationships, not only the love of nature but also the love between two people. Love is gentle, tender, and sublime just as the descending leaf and rising sun are. By means of his poetry, he was able to captivate and expose the splendorous qualities of nature, which become an integral part of man's emotions when he allows images to stir and elevate his soul. Byron understood that in this day and age of progress and cement, man could not afford to ignore the thirst of his inner self, which he inherently searches to quench.

Lance strongly believed poetry was very essential in a world replete of crime, greed, war, indifference, selfishness, and narrow-mindedness. Poetry was so profound and everlasting, and few people cherished its meaning or wanted to understand it. This emotion often vexed Lance, but he knew Byron and other poets throughout the centuries must have shared these same frustrations. Poetry probably evolved out of man's need to separate oneself from the demands of everyday living. This expression could only be appreciated in the quiet moments of solitude when one sat in the darkness of a room in a cozy chair under the light of a friendly lamp, where one could read and experience the moving force of its verse.

As Lance was lost in his thoughts, the name "Lance Sullivan" resonated through the bus station. Mr. Brown, the man sent to pick him up, finally arrived. "How are you doing Lance? I'm sorry you had to wait so long, but I had a flat tire on the way."

Lance was happy to see him. "I'm doing fine, sir. I had a nice flight, and I am very grateful to be here. I'm looking forward to camp, and I can't wait to see Walt Frazier shoot some hoops."

Mr. Brown loaded Lance's bag into the van and shut the door. Lance noticed his protruding nose, shaped like a hook. He also had a beer belly, which hung over his belt buckle. His thick coke bottled glasses were blotched by fingerprints. The grease from changing his tire probably added another layer of grime to his lenses. Lance wondered if his "view of the world" was as blotchy as looking out a car window on a misty day. Lance was intrigued by his red and brown plaid flannel shirt, which contrasted significantly with his striped grey polyester pants. Lance searched for a wedding band on his left hand but did not see one. However, he did notice that Mr. Brown's nails were bitten down to the quick of his fingers. Mr. Brown's good demeanor did not match his grooming habits. "Is this your first trip to New York? If it is, you made a wise decision to come to Monticello. It's really rustic and peaceful out here in this part of the country."

Lance responded, "Yes, I've been to New York before. I came to Manhattan about four years ago when I was about eleven years old. But, you are right. It's beautiful here, and this is my first time in Monticello."

"I've lived here about twenty years, and I don't plan on leaving. I have a farm just about ten miles from camp headquarters, and I love the tranquility of living out in the wilderness."

"It sounds like you have it all figured out."

The countryside was breathtaking. Huge pine and elm trees filled the roadsides with an abundance of mountains and hills layering the horizon. The air was crisp and fresh, and frequently, deer appeared hidden behind the trees and green foliage. And of course, Lance saw a multitude of rabbits and squirrels roaming around and frolicking in the warmth of the early afternoon sun. His excitement amplified as he thought about spending the next two weeks in this idyllic place.

When Lance arrived to the camp's administrative building, he was assigned a room. He was given a key, and Mr. Brown drove him to his dormitory. For the next fourteen days, Lance would be sleeping and hanging out in room 206 of Bear Hall. A bunch of boys were unloading their bags and luggage from cars parked in the parking lot. Lance carried his duffle bag up the stairs to his room. He opened the door, and it was evident his roommate had not arrived yet. Each camper would share a room with another boy. The room was simply decorated without any fancy frills. It contained one large commodious brown desk with two sets of dressers with three drawers each. The chair belonging to the desk had a torn cushion, exposing the foam under its vinyl cover. On the opposite side of the room, there was a bunk bed with a ladder extending from the floor to the top exposed mattress. The beds were covered meticulously with white linen and a grey blanket tucked under each pillow. There were two large windows overlooking a dense thicket of trees cushioning the building. Lance felt a sense of calmness and security as he set his bag on the bottom bed.

As he bent over to unzip his bag and begin unpacking, the door creaked as it opened behind him. A tall sleek looking boy stood at the entrance of the room. They introduced themselves immediately by shaking hands.

"Hey, my name is Lance. What's yours?"

"What's going on? I'm James. It's nice to meet you. I guess we will be roommates for a couple of weeks."

"Yeah, I can't wait to learn some tips from Walt Frazier. He's one heck of a basketball player."

"There's no doubt. He definitely is a bad ass."

James and Lance continued to talk and get to know each other. Lance decided to take the lower bunk, since it would be easier for James, who was much taller, to get in the top bunk bed. After they finished unpacking their stuff, it was time for dinner. They both walked to the cafeteria. James was born in San Francisco, California, and he was in the ninth grade. He was interested in basketball, but the main reason he came to camp was to get away from his parents who constantly fought. He also wanted to improve his game so that he could try out for the junior varsity team next year. James had a crush on this girl named Patsy back home, who had big tits and was really into jocks. She would be trying out for the junior varsity cheerleading squad next year.

Outdoors the temperature was fairly cool compared to the stifling weather Lance had experienced in Columbia, Missouri. It was about sixty-five degrees. Since Monticello was located in a mountainous region with an abundance of pine and elm trees, a continuous breeze flowed from the heart of the thicket cooling them off. The odiferous smell from the abundance of trees carried by the friendly breeze was tantalizing. Lance took a deep breath as he soaked up the relaxing ambiance. As they walked, Lance's mind began to drift into the future, and he foresaw the time when he was enrolled at the university taking college courses in Texas. Friedrich Wilhelm Nietzsche's philosophy, the 19th century German writer, had appealed to him.

The "eternal recurrence" was a concept developed by Nietzsche in his writings. The concept referred to the cycle of nature and life. When one living being died, another one was born. There was no finality to life because this inexplicable cycle repeated itself continuously. Henry David Thoreau, the American 19th century essayist and philosopher, also understood this idea, but he examined it from a different perspective. Thoreau wrote about the seasons and how they changed in his book *On Walden Pond*. Each season had its own characteristics and personality; they all evolved and revealed themselves throughout the course of the year. The flowers and trees would blossom in the spring, slowly bringing nature back to life. In the summer, all animals and plants would come to full fruition as animals scurried about, and farmers harvested their crops. The fall began its metamorphosis as the leaves began to change colors, and birds would begin to migrate south. The winter embraced man with its cold breath of finality, reminding man of nature's purging. During this season, many plants and animals became dormant. This was a time for reflection in which nature, through its natural cycle, taught man to search within to discover the inner truths of life. Nietzsche and Thoreau took time to peruse and ponder the meaning of life and its cycles. Life is the inevitable confinement man tries to avoid and run from, but he can never escape its presence since he lives within its walls.

Lance asked for chicken fried steak as he walked down the food aisle of the cafeteria, and James ordered macaroni and cheese with green beans. There was a lot of commotion because it was the first day of camp. Everyone was excited about being here. The enthusiasm saturated the air as the boys and staff talked and became acquainted with one another in this new environment. The cafeteria was commodious, and the large windows provided an excellent view of the campgrounds with its bucolic panoramic background. When Lance and James sat down, they could not ignore the unspoiled setting which was totally captivating. There was a thicket of trees in the background of an outdoors complex, which included ten exterior basketball courts. To the north of the courts, there were four tennis courts. There was also a swimming pool, a 400-meter track, and weight room. In addition, there was a gymnasium housing four large basketball courts. To the left of this complex, there was a small lake attracting many campers who were interested in water skiing, windsurfing, canoeing, and other water activities. This camp was definitely a jock's paradise. Lance liked the fact that even though this was primarily a basketball camp, they offered opportunities for everyone to participate in other sports.

Advancing to another nostalgic moment in time, Lance would look back at this experience at the Kutsher's Sports Academy, and he would understand the significance and compulsion of North Americans who valued and loved sports. The time he spent at the camp was fruitful because not only did he improve his skills, but he also learned to love and appreciate the game of basketball. However, Lance believed this experience might have been detrimental to some kids who were coerced to play basketball or other sports by their parents. Parents oftentimes tried to relive their repressed dreams and ambitions through the lives of their offspring. Many times, it seemed like the focus of these academies for many adults was to prepare kids to play competitive ball at the college and possibly professional levels rather than emphasize the joy of sport and play that could last a lifetime.

Lance was lucky because his parents did not coerce him to participate in sports. John firmly believed it was essential to expose children to sports, music, and other activities in which the child might have an interest. Once Lance did choose to participate in sports, primarily basketball and track, John wanted to make sure Lance truly enjoyed the sports he played. According to John, sports represented one of the many *vehicles* by which a person could learn about life. John stressed the importance of not becoming obsessed by winning and being number one. The true principal of sport should help a person to cultivate, stimulate, and develop his body and mind. Sports should be taught as an art form similar to music, ballet, art, literature, and other forms of knowledge. A person could foster an inner strength and understanding about himself and the world surrounding him through sports.

When Lance specifically looked back at this experience and the time he devoted and still dedicates training for triathlons, he realized the majority of participants and spectators did not share his philosophy. Unfortunately, money and big businesses dominate the world of athletic competition in the United States. The media has made great strides in promoting and covering sport events in our country and around the world; however, it glorifies sports and super athletes to such an excessive extent that one sometimes feels like only those select few can really gain from its recompense. In a way, this is good because many of these athletes are good role models for younger kids. But, few advertisements promote sports as a means for developing and strengthening the interconnectedness between mind, body, and soul for all people who choose to participate in the athletic arena. This simple truth allows a person to live to his fullest potential. Dr. George Sheehan, the famous cardiologist and writer of the 20th century, once said, "There is an athlete in all of us, waiting to be challenged." Society and the media seek professionals and winners, the products of a materialistic society, which worships success and money above the psyche and transcendental.

Lance believes schools should instruct kids to pursue athletics as a means for developing the whole person, mentally and physically.

Sports should be introduced at an early age as a lifestyle by which one can lead a healthy and productive life. They should always be played in the spirit of fair competition. Winning should not be the immediate and final result of competition. Success should not be determined by how fast a person runs, or by how many touchdowns someone scores; rather it should be measured by the effort the athlete expends. The essence of competition is striving for perfection and sharing the effort through competition, not solely to establish who is faster or stronger. It should fulfill the need to extend oneself to his physical and spiritual limits. An athlete should strive for the personal victory in which he overcomes his own fears and limitations as he attempts to surpass them. He must learn to face and confront these inner challenges on a daily basis. Humbleness and meekness should be the end result of any sport because with this presence of mind, one transcends and becomes a part of nature. Arrogance and bombastic attitudes gained through competition separate and alienate men from themselves and their surroundings.

Carl Gustav Jung, the famous 19th century psychiatrist and philosopher from Switzerland, states in his book *Answer to Job*: "'Physical is not the only criterion of truth: there are also 'psychic' truths which can neither be explained nor proved nor contested in any physical way." Lance believed Jung understood those truths, which go beyond the physical, the ability of the athlete to perform. In the West and probably in the East, man is amazed by the physical, by what he sees with his eyes. The scientist can evaluate, study, and explain the mechanics of the human body. But, has man taken the time to study and comprehend the "psychic" aspect of the athlete? Lance was sure it had been studied; however, this type of research may not be as popular or as interesting to the general population partaking as spectators or athletes in a given sport. In a competitive arena, the athlete comes into contact with his conscious and subconscious self. He explores the realm of his physical capabilities and shortcomings sensing an inexplicable satisfaction, which cannot be defined by words, because he knows and comes to understand himself. He ascertains and acts upon a substantiated ecstasy and joy, which motivates him to live fully.

Sports had always fascinated Lance because they serve as an exercise for him to ponder, think, and play with ideas. He would never dismiss Dr. Sheehan's words in reference to running: "There are as many reasons for running as there are days in the year, years in any life. But mostly I run because I am an animal and a child, an artist, and a saint. So too are you. Find your own play, your own self-renewing compulsion, and you will become the person you are meant to be." Lance sought this balance in life, that special equilibrium between mind and body, the physical and psychic. Once this equitable state is achieved at an individual level, it could transcend collectively, relating directly to all aspects of life: politics, economics, humanitarian causes, religious affiliations, and other areas common among all nations and people of the world.

God had obviously understood the gift he had bestowed upon man: the ability to reason and wonder. God has created the animal, which relies on instinct for survival, but the animal cannot think. Man, on the other hand, relies on his instincts and ability to reason. Through science, he discovered the many marvels of the universe. However, science could not explain everything. Man is incapable of rationally comprehending all the secrets of life. He cannot rely on science exclusively to explain the creation of the world, nor can he manipulate its hypothetical conclusions to overcome death. Man has learned to believe and have faith in God, or a higher power, only if he chooses to do so. Some have chosen not to believe, not to consider the unknown mysteries and miracles of death. Death scares man, and he doesn't want to face its uncertainties. Unfortunately, man will never conquer death from a *non-spiritual perspective*; therefore, he will not control the unknown. Man must look into himself as he seeks to comprehend the greatness and miraculous nature of this world.

Lance's mind continued to drift as he thought about the crisis in the Persian Gulf (1989-1990). How do sports and the thoughts of Jung and Plato relate to the conflict between Iraq and the rest of the world? Saddam Hussein believed he was right in invading Kuwait appalling other countries with his intrusive disregard for others. It is obvious that power and greed have disrupted the balance between mind and body not only on an individual yet collective scale as well.

Inevitably, this human condition affects all people and nations throughout the world. Tyrants have always existed (Hitler, Stalin, Mussolini, Louis XIV, and a multitude of other miscreants), and they will continue to exist and disrupt the equilibrium between man and society.

The human psyche must be nourished by religion, philosophy, or spirituality, which guide and instruct men to live in harmony with their individual selves and each other, but sometimes man's zeal turns into fanaticism, corrupting his beliefs to satisfy his egotistical needs. What is lacking in our world today is the ability to dialogue and discuss our differences with each other worldwide with tolerance, respect, and sensitivity for other languages, perspectives, and traditions. If there is no conversation, there will be no peace on earth. It was Lance's view that cultures have deviated from their spiritual paths; as a result, people have veered away from the necessary dialogues required to compassionately understand one another.

Peace comes from the realization that no one is perfect; therefore, no one comprehends the whole truth about his life and the afterlife.

Nations and governments need to stop brainwashing their citizens into thinking that their way of living is the best and only way. People should be afforded the freedom and space to question their beliefs and suppositions of the world so as to be open to other views and ways of life, which are different, but not necessarily better or worse from their own. No individual culture is superior or inferior to another but equal in the eyes of a loving and merciful God whose seed lives in all of us. Men need to look beyond the physical, whether it is an athlete in competition or a nation with superior war arsenals, to transcend to a higher level of subsistence and regard for all lives.

It is easy for man to look at the external aspects of his life as he ignores his internal makeup. Politics and government are external to man's well-being because they do not affect his immediate health and emotions. Politics can affect a person and society, but it cannot completely control the soul of the individual. A ruthless tyrant, who subordinates the liberty and rights of its people, controls many societies. Nevertheless, can this type of ruthless dictator truly control the mind and body of its people?

It seems like it is one of the most difficult things for men to apprehend. Man often ignores his "internal" and natural needs because he is distracted by the commotion that surrounds him. In this modern and advanced age, there are so many distractions (work, education, leisure, chores, and others) that occupy our time. The pressures of modern day life and the frenetic activities that enthrall us throughout the day leave us devoid of the quiet and reflective spaces for solitude. When there is no time for meditating and being alone, a person cannot grow and "nurture" his spiritual mind and body. Man needs to force himself away from his home and workplace to find a reticent place, whether it be a park or nature trail, where he can walk and be alone with himself, his thoughts, and bucolic surroundings.

Nature is the one place in the world where man can "find himself." With its consoling beauty, he can renew his ties to life, himself, and society because, here, he returns to the harmonious state he craves instinctively. God created the flora, fauna, and man for a purpose. God must have known that man would need a place to return to, a place full of trees, vast oceans, birds, flowers, and other natural gems for man's recreation. Without this form of retreat, man could not reacquaint himself with this truth. What is the meaning of life? Each individual can only answer this question for himself. For this reason man must separate himself from his external artificial ambiance to enter into his *mundo ensimismado* (internal world) where he can become saturated by God's love, inciting him to love not only self but others as well.

Chapter 4

THOUGHTFUL REFLECTIONS

When man moves away from the understanding of oneself and advances into the technological world of our modern age, controlled by computers and satellites, the "details" of life are lost in the quagmire of information. Therefore, it is good to remind ourselves of David Thoreau's sagacious words: "The world is frittered away with detail ... simplify, simplify." If people of the world would cogitate and heed to this advice, peace might predominate across the world. If countries could learn to appreciate each other's culture, religion, and language; if nations would become less industrial and progressive, polluting the oceans, rivers, and air; if nations would be less materialistic; and if men would not concern themselves so much with property, money, fame, and work, there would be fewer details to tend to in life. Technological advancement is necessary for the betterment of society, which improves science, education, and employment opportunities, but when technology distracts man and replaces the simplicity of living with its complexity, this is counterproductive. We live in the 21st century where people are more attentive to their smart phones and have lost touch with their own souls and those of others.

Lance thought Thoreau made sense. There are certain things man has to live with and accept in his daily life. Some things, such as work, nuclear arms, and industries cannot be dismissed exclusively; however, we can attribute less significance to them. These facets of our life do not occupy every moment of our existence. If man could learn to divert his attention from time to time from these concerns and focus on the true meaning of life, such as peace, solitude, and oneness with nature, the other components would not be ignored but esteemed in their proper perspective. Nevertheless, if man chooses to disregard the search for unity and separateness, he will become dissatisfied and disappointed with his life. Man needs time to reflect and walk quietly along nature's path, so he can listen, smell, and touch the hidden treasures therein. Men should determine to acknowledge Thoreau's advice to disentangle life.

After lunch, Lance and James returned to their room and finished unpacking their bags. They talked about their hometowns and family. James was from Baton Rouge, Louisiana, and he had two brothers and one sister. His father was an engineer working for an oil drilling company in New Iberia, La. His family chose not to live in New Iberia because there was not a broad selection of schools to choose from for their children. James had been playing basketball for several years now. He was going to be a sophomore in high school next year, and he wanted to improve his skills. He was short at 5'11" and was interested in bettering his ball handling, shooting, and passing abilities. He played point guard, which is the same position Lance played. They were about the same size. James's favorite player was Pistol Petey Maravich, who played college ball at LSU in the late 1960s and later professional ball for the New Orleans Jazz.

At two o'clock in the afternoon, Jeff Robinson, the dorm leader and supervisor, knocked on Lance's door to remind the boys of the all campus meeting to be held in the main gymnasium at 2:30 that afternoon. Jeff introduced himself to Lance and James. He was about 6'4", and he ducked his head under the door as he entered the room. The boys were astonished by his size and build. They came to find out that Jeff spent innumerable hours on the basketball court and in the weight room. He was from Indiana, and he was a sophomore at DePauw University. He had been playing basketball since the eighth grade. Jeff also wanted to revamp his game because he had a good chance of starting next year as a point guard. This past season he was a backup guard, and although he did not register a lot of time on the court at first, he played quite a bit toward the end of the season, averaging fourteen points and five assists per game. Rollo Gutiérrez, the starting guard for his team, had twisted his ankle allotting him more time in the game.

At 2:15 p.m. Lance and James left their room as they walked down the hill to the gymnasium. All of the boys from the various dorms migrated towards the large complex housing the four basketball courts. It was as if all of them were on a pilgrimage to the mecca to meet some supreme being. Lance could feel the excitement in the air as they briskly strolled down the hill. Some of the boys were carrying their basketballs, and others were wearing sweatbands of multiple colors around their wrists with a multitude donning headbands and kneepads. Some of them looked like manikins, who had just escaped from the nearest sports department store, with all of the sports paraphernalia they were wearing. The cool guys wore blue jean shorts and a basic white T-shirt with their white or black high top Converse tennis shoes. Lance could sense the eagerness of the boys and staff who were ready to begin the activities. He intuited this was going to be an invaluable experience, one that would remain impregnated in his mind for years to come. After all, it's not often that one envisions a herd of "marionettes" blindly following each other to a musty gymnasium perfumed by the odors distilled by jock straps and pungent socks.

There was an abundance of bleachers set up inside the gymnasium. The noise of the campers walking, talking, and sitting down resonated throughout the gym. Bob J. Waters, a well-known professional basketball coach, stood on a stage and began to speak. He had been coaching for approximately thirty-five years, and he was the ultimate guru of the game. He would be everyone's spiritual leader for the next two weeks.

Obviously, he was the head coach of the camp, and he overlooked all the activities and established the camp rules. The staff members and other coaches received their daily instructions from him.

The campers sensed the confidence and expertise behind the words of this great coach. He was a rather small man, but his deep thick voice reverberated across the gym as he spoke. The other coaches and staff really respected him. Lance did not know if he coached any team participating in a N.B.A. championship this year; however, he exuded the confidence of an outstanding leader. One would think that he and his teams had won several titles. Basically, Coach Waters described to the campers the different activities and facilities, which were available to them. He also reiterated the fact that they would have many opportunities to learn about basketball because some of the best coaches and players in the country would be working with them throughout their two-week stay.

Everyone became mesmerized when Coach Waters began to speak about the dynamics of basketball. He said it was advantageous to have big hands and long fingers to control the ball. Lance thought about this and agreed, noting that obviously hands were important for mastering the fundamentals of the game: shooting, dribbling, passing the ball, and playing defense. He pointed out several exercises to stretch out the fingers in an attempt to strengthen the whole hand.

Lance's mind began to drift again when he thought about the value of hands not only for basketball, but everything we do in life. For the poet, the hands represented the extension of his soul reaching out with pen in hand to etch on paper the precious truths of life. This special link gives life to the poet's images and metaphors. A philosopher might have observed: "The hand gives life to the poet's verses; thus, provides the sustenance of his own existence."

Lance reminisced about an eighth grade class he was teaching one summer. On a particular day he was showing a movie about the human body and its multifarious functions. The movie presented the various psychological and biological functions of the body. After discussing the internal systems of the body, the mechanical and external movements were depicted. The hand was considered to be the most versatile part of the human body. A person could use the hand for multiple activities: grasping, releasing, writing, and an amalgamation of other activities.

There is no doubt man would be handicapped without the use of his hands. It would be remiss not to mention Leonardo da Vinci, the renowned Italian Renaissance artist from the 16th century, and the detailed hands he painted in one of his most well-known works, the *Last Supper*. The attention given to the hands of Christ and the twelve disciples is truly masterful and expressive. Jesus' right palm is positioned downwards with his left one upwards, and this juxtaposition could have several meanings. It occurred to Lance that his hands illustrated the grace of God who descended to earth in the human form of his Son (hand facing downwards) and would soon ascend back to heaven to return to his side (hand facing upwards). Furthermore, the hands of the apostles characterize and convey love, compassion, confusion, vulnerability, and a multitude of other sentiments, which all honor Jesus in their last moment together.

That summer Lance learned quite a bit about basketball and life. There were many basketball teams at the camp, and his squad, named the Bulls, did fairly well even though Lance felt they could have done better. They won five games and lost five, whereas James's team did a little better with six wins and four losses. Their coach Jeff gave both Lance and James many invaluable tips. He taught Lance and James how to dribble between their legs as they walked. This drill developed their ability to handle the ball fluidly. Jeff also taught them how to dribble behind their backs.

Although Jeff did not dribble that much behind his back and in between his legs during games, he believed these exercises helped him to develop balance, speed, good reflexes, and dexterity with both his hands. Being able to respond to different types of defenses required the ability to dribble equally well with both hands. In the end, sports is not about defining one's success by the number of wins and losses, but Jeff instilled the value of basketball being a representation of the challenges one faces in life. Each day presents a new beginning for honing one's skills professionally and spiritually to adequately confront the ups and downs of living. The discipline, practice, and love of improving one's life are the key factors to help one another progress in a group effort, much like a team of five.

Besides playing a lot of basketball, James and Lance spent a lot of time together communing and hanging out. On several occasions after dinner, they walked through the woods towards a creek to sit, talk, and smoke cigarettes. It was a time of reflection and growth where they could get away from the daily activities and enjoy a moment of detachment and relaxation. They knew that smoking was bad for them, and it would probably prevent their fingers and hands from getting any bigger. Nevertheless, at that blithe moment, they only cared about relishing the intangible gathering of youth. They laughed as they thought about their hands shrinking smoking the growth impairing Winston Lights. When they inhaled, Lance thought about Puerto Rico and his best friend and "big brother" who he truly missed. The camaraderie between friends is priceless, and he realized that absence makes the heart fonder of someone like Alex.

Lance continued to think, now, that he was sitting at his desk looking back on life. In graduate school, he remembered seeing the movie "Dead Poet's Society," which really inspired him. Robin Williams played an excellent role as an English teacher at a private prep high school for boys. He was a very liberal teacher who broke down the barriers in education created by conservative, stagnant, and conforming administrators and teachers. Williams taught his classes in a very nonconventional, a Ralph Waldo Emerson manner, so as to inspire students to learn and really experience their education in a fun and meaningful way. On the first day of class, Williams stands on his desk and asks his students to open their books to the preface. Then, he asks them to tear out the first page and the remaining ones of the prologue written by some PhD, who explicated a certain guideline for reading, studying, and understanding poetry and English literature.

William's actions portrayed his feelings and opinions regarding the study of poetry and education believing teachers do not need a PhD to elucidate poetry to students. Each person can look within and search for the appropriate meaning of each verse as he interprets and untangles it with his own mind. Professors have been telling students for years how to read and analyze poetry; now, it was time for students to take responsibility as they decipher its meaning, freeing themselves of the anal retentive ways of learning established by the present educational system. Based on this creative paradigm, students are engaged, and the lyrical verse changes them in a meaningful way because they become the conduits of transformation by living and breathing each metaphor.

Lance felt very strongly about the deficiencies in the educational system; especially, the fact that most institutions did not develop the creativity and thinking capacities of their students. Lance remembered reading the book *Motivation and Personality*, written by Abraham H. Maslow, who supported Lance's beliefs about education when he stated: "[Education] gives [an individual] a set of prefabricated spectacles with which to look at the world in every aspect, e.g., what to believe, what to like, what to approve of, what to feel guilty about." This really bothered Lance because he felt like an educator had a right to teach students how to think and look at the world through their own eyes. When education does not disseminate and value this style of teaching, it confines and subjects the student to the will of others, which stifles his creativity and imagination.

Lance thought some more about education and its effect on society and its divergent institutions. He recalled attending a Sunday service at a Baptist Church in which the minister was giving a sermon based on a book from the Old Testament. The preacher was making a point about how man attempts to set his own guidelines and wishes to follow his own will. Upon reflecting on a recent trip he took to Europe, he observed that someone had painted the words "God is dead" on a wall. It was signed with Nietzsche's name. Someone disapproved of the quote painting over the word God and replacing it with Nietzsche; thus, the phrase now read: "Nietzsche is dead." God signed it.

As Lance listened to the sermon, this overt, yet interesting, statement puzzled him. It surprised Lance at first that the preacher did not discuss much about Friedrich Nietzsche and who he was. Lance was almost certain that few in the congregation had ever heard of this German philosopher before. Anyway, Lance believed the preacher should have given more background information about Nietzsche if he chose to quote him in his sermon. By providing some biographical details, people could develop their own opinion of him. Lance understood that this quote could have a different meaning. One of the main questions philosophers pose is: "What is reality, and what isn't?" In Lance's opinion, the next important question should be: "Who is God?" This is a very difficult question to answer; however, Lance regarded it as one everyone should ponder. Furthermore, Nietzsche influenced many free thinkers and intelligentsias in Europe during the years leading up to World War II. He supported the socialist movement comprised of anarchists and nihilists who were tired of the aristocracy and ruling classes controlling and oppressing the masses. Nietzsche advocated the ideas of the "superman" during a time of spiritual crisis, especially in Germany. He professed that man could take control of his own spiritual and political needs, since the state and ruling classes, who place their faith in God, were only watching out for their own interests. Unfortunately, many churches, regardless of denomination, did not encourage its people to reflect on the existence of God from an individual perspective. Lance believed Nietzsche was trying to get people to think for themselves about their government and personal beliefs instead of allowing the State and Church to think and believe in God for them.

Furthermore, it is possible Nietzsche meant to say that God is dead in terms of what the logic and reason of the human mind can comprehend. God is too complex for man to fully grasp by reason alone. We, the human race, are a creation of God according to some believers; therefore, we must rely on faith to fully attempt to understand his greatness. Faith is something, which cannot be delineated by the finite limitations of logical reasoning, but this should not discourage man from seeking the truth. To fully grasp the truth, it's necessary to question it like Nietzsche has done. If one doesn't question God and his greatness, how can one ever come to fully know him?

It totally vexed Lance when the preacher made this observation or "judgment" without truly knowing much about Nietzsche's work, or so it seemed, since he did not elaborate on the subject. Lance pondered some more, and he realized all men, whether church leaders, teachers, businessmen, politicians, and others make unjustified judgments. This is an inherent part of man's fallible human nature, which binds him to his imperfections. He who judges is an imperfect man; as a result, he who does not judge is following God's command. Man's imperfections should constantly remind him of his weakness. Realizing this, man should constantly look within himself and determine whether he is making a judgment or an observation based on research and personal opinions, or whether he observes without previous evidence or knowledge. However, one must also understand that regardless of the amount of time he researches a subject, he still falls short of knowing the absolute truth in a given area, not only because of the constraints of reason but also because of one's imperfect nature.

Lance's thoughts kept him company as he sat under the shade of the elm tree and took a few puffs from his cigarette. People who made the habit of forming unjustified discernments not only poisoned their thinking process by basing their opinion on insubstantial information, but they also stifled their ability to comprehend complex issues. This ability to question and think about ideas is essential for nourishing the soul. Lance knew deep down inside that he was as supercilious as anyone else. Life is a perplexing experiment in which our thoughts can either free us from its complexity or enslave us.

These contradictions constantly bewildered Lance as he thought about life. He imagined God sitting on a rocking chair on some distant mountain in the celestial heavens looking at Lance and the rest of the human race with an amusing smile. God had devised an experiment in which he had given man the chance to live an abundant life, yet man chose to listen to himself, ignoring His advice. Since man chose to be guided by his ability to reason, man would suffer throughout his life. The pendulum of his existence would swing from happy to melancholic experiences, depression to ecstasy, and from failure to success. Men would constantly strive to learn all there is to know about life. Some would become educated in science, literature, philosophy, and other fields; conversely, many would ignore the simple truths of the world. Others neglected the concerns of the intellectual world living in a state of indifference to their surroundings.

A single ray of glittering sunlight filtered through the shadow of the enormous oak tree and vegetation surrounding Lance. The stillness and separateness of the afternoon comforted him immensely. His thoughts became his most intimate friends. The leaves, trees, sunlight, humid ground, and the animals, which befriended him, mystified him. He imagined himself gamboling through the branches, seeing the crevices and irregular grooves of the wood close up.

In this imaginary state, he came across Pedro, an ant, who was waiting outside of a beauty salon where his girlfriend Rosa was getting her hair done. Lance learned that Pedro and Rosa were journeying through the countryside of this expansive tree. They were on their way to the *mecca* where they would congregate with a multitude of ants from all over the world. Here they would listen to music and several speakers from diverse cultures and nations. Lance also discovered that in the ant community everyone spoke each other's language. Children were taught all the languages of the world along with the history of each country.

In earlier centuries, there were many wars among neighboring nations, but now, everyone in the global ant civilization lived in everlasting peace working for the common good. There was plenty of food for all people, and there was no monetary or tax system imposed on any of the communities. Previously, kingdoms and nations fought for land for their people. Individuals wanted their own property, but this only created greed and hatred because the desire to own became greater. The leaders of the world convened and realized this attitude only created dissension and rifts between nations; therefore, the leaders agreed to form a *world association* in which every individual and family were allotted a small portion of land. This method proved successful because no one was deprived of owning property. In addition, groups from around the world shared their religious beliefs, which ranged from Buddhism, Hinduism, Islam, Judaism, Christianity, and many other religions. Once a year, the multifarious ant nations from around the world congregated at the mecca, the designated place for their annual meeting, which happened to be at the apex of this majestic tree. Here they shared their beliefs and renewed their bonds to one another. The love they conveyed to one another was overpowering. Lance's thoughts returned to the real world where the imagination and its dreamlike qualities seemed unreal. As he contemplated life, he knew he would never know the complete truth concerning the existence of man, which temporarily saddened him. Nevertheless, his thoughts assuaged him that God was nearby, and his love extended to all mankind even amidst the suffering and misunderstandings in the world.

Suddenly, Lance heard a voice calling him from a distance. "Lance, Lance. Where are you?" James was calling him from the road adjacent to the thick brush. Lance replied: "I'm over here James." James ran up to Lance and told him Walt Frazier would be conducting an exhibition on shooting jump shots at 10 a.m. Lance was overwhelmed with emotion because Walt was his all-time favorite player. Frazier made a name for himself as an excellent ball handler with a picture perfect jump shot. He also played great defense. Lance knew he was one of the best to have ever played the game.

The swooshing sound of the basketball falling gracefully through the hoop silenced the capacious gymnasium filled with approximately four hundred boys and staff, who sat in awe, observing the performance of the magician. He dribbled the ball effortlessly and gracefully jumped straight up in the air releasing the ball from the tip of his fingers. Lance would never forget his controlled and fluid motion. Lance sensed a certain joy as he watched Walt take each shot. This man had mastered a skill, which he executed flawlessly. Lance realized that it wasn't important whether a person played basketball or wrote poetry; however, the implication was to choose a career or hobby in life, which instilled a certain joy once it was deftly perfected. Part of the rapture is acquired in the struggle and effort required to achieve proficiency knowing that the intention may or may not lead to success or fame.

Walt Frazier learned the value of hard work and determination, but he also must have known the principle of choosing an activity in which he felt totally free and gained much pleasure and satisfaction. Success is relative. In Walt's case, he was able to become a legend on the basketball court, but more importantly, achievement should be measured solely by the enjoyment one derives from the hobby or career one chooses.

Lance really enjoyed himself at the Kutsher's Sports Academy that summer. When it terminated, he would fly back to San Juan, Puerto Rico to spend a couple of weeks with his family and friends. Afterwards, he would return to Kansas City, Missouri where he would spend a year with his aunt and uncle. He sat in the window seat of a Delta Airline's Jumbo Jet 747 looking out into the clouds. Totally relaxed, he listened to the Beatles on his headset and ruminated about the two weeks he spent at camp in Monticello. He had a great time and learned quite a bit about basketball. He was impressed by the one pickup game he saw between a few professional players who were visiting the camp. The one player who stuck out in his mind was Charlie Scott, a player for the Phoenix Suns. Charlie was extremely quick, and his ability to jump and hang in the air was truly unprecedented. The talent of Walt Frazier, Charlie Scott, and other players like them totally amazed him.

The big plane finally arrived to Puerto Rico. Lance was very excited to see his parents, since he had not seen them for a couple of months. The tropical heat was very comforting and calming as he seethed in the salty breeze from the soothing Caribbean Sea. Lance and John talked about basketball and the camp for several hours while Josephine prepared a sumptuous dinner. She prepared his favorite dish, goulash and chili in cornbread, and for dessert they ate her favorite creamy and delectable cheesecake. It was also nice to see Karla who had stayed in Puerto Rico basking in the sun, playing tennis, and going to parties with her Cuban and Puerto Rican friends. On the island, especially during the summer months, parties were ubiquitous. Someone either had a birthday party, a *quinceañera* (celebrating the beginning of womanhood at the tender age of fifteen), or a *fiesta* just to get together for fun. People enjoyed hanging out, listening to music, dancing, and socializing.

Being back in Puerto Rico was a pleasant change because life was not as hurried as in the States. People were not consumed by strict work schedules at the expense of other things. The basic island attitude was centered on the proverbial saying, "Déjalo para mañana". (Leave it for tomorrow.) Puerto Ricans took more time to be with friends and family and preferred to work at a leisurely pace. Like most people they enjoyed going to the beach or mountains in the countryside. Strolling down the nostalgic narrow cobblestoned streets of Old San Juan, the ancient citadel the Spaniards built when they occupied Puerto Rico in the 16th century, was a rite of passage for most Puerto Ricans. Old San Juan was replete with colonial homes and overhanging verandas jetting out into the streets. Most of the homes painted in pastel hues provided a fresh transparency complementing the brightness of a clear day. Inside many of them, there were roofless patios with fountains, plants, and bouquets of flowers exposed to the open air. In addition, there was an abundance of shops, restaurants, bars, and historical remnants of the past: El Morro (the Spanish fort), churches, and statues. Old San Juan and the island with its everlasting charm would always entice Lance to its shores and foster a profound love.

On his first night home, Lance, Karla, and his parents talked, dined, and laughed. They really reveled in each other's company, and they were mirthful to be together again. The following morning Lance and John got up early and went to the beach. John would normally stretch, run one mile down the beach, and swim in the ocean for about fifteen minutes. Lance was going to run six miles in approximately forty minutes. The blissful and tranquil predawn light slowly emerged reflecting from the blue ocean as waves simultaneously descended and crashed lightly on the sand. The bubbling white froth comforted Lance as he began to run by the edge of the shore. He was overtaken by a sudden euphoria created by the ocean, wind, sea, sun, and azure skies; their intimacy stirred the tranquility and happiness within. Nature is the object of man's jubilation, and without its renewing qualities, man would decompose in the chaos and confusion of the world. It was impossible to ignore the sublime reality of its crux, which filtered through the eyes and invigorated the soul. The sun with its *perpetual paintbrush* created images of aberrant tones with its golden touch; thus, it withheld the eternal light of God's wisdom in its representation. Lance would always venerate these detached moments on the beach where he could permeate within his inner sanctuary of completeness and serenity.

Lance would never forget the events that shaped his past. One day during lunch, Lance browsed through the *Austin American-Statesman* newspaper. He began to read an article about two Russian chess wizards, Garry Kasparov and Anatoly Karpov, who were competing against each other for the championship in 1990. Kasparov, the founder of a Soviet Democratic Party, had declared he was playing under the flag of the

Republic rather than the Soviet Union. He was quoted as saying, "I have two loves, democracy for Russia and chess." The first game of their opening match, which lasted approximately five hours, ended in a draw. This match was held at the Hudson Theatre in Manhattan where tickets for seven hundred seats sold for $25, $50, and $100. Kasparov, at the age of twenty-two, had defeated Karpov in 1985, ending Karpov's ten year reign as champion. Karpov, at the age of thirty-nine, was trying to regain his title as he challenged his nemesis for the first time in three years. It was the first world championship held in the United States since 1907. The first twelve games would be played in New York, and the remaining twelve in Lyon, France, beginning on November 12.

It amazed Lance that a chess game could last five hours. Russians seemed to really revere the game. Based on his experiences, he concluded there were not many Americans who played chess, at least not among the people he had met. Lance wondered if the considerable number of Russians playing the game could lead one to assess that their culture, under the oppression of communism (1912-1991) for so many years, established a vacuum for the insightful game of chess as if society as a whole closely examined its next move against this colossal foe. Could it be possible that in a democracy, inspired by materialism, men, because of their power to buy and consume, are more inclined to purchase and do things? Are democratic nations also drawn away from their thoughts by television, sports, cars, houses, and other material distractions? Whereas, in a communist country, this type of freedom to act and, moreover, to spend money does not exist. Most people in the Soviet Union, excluding members of the *nomenklatura* (the privileged class), could not afford to *spawn* their own destiny because their government limited them. Waiting in line to receive the staples (sugar, bread, milk, and meat) for survival is not the same as having the freedom to enter a *gargantuan* grocery store at any time without waiting long. There, one could choose to purchase from a plethora of items, ranging from Q-tips and other hygienic necessities to the most exotic fruit imported from abroad along with a fresh variety of food and other items. Was it possible, then, that in Russia most people were forced to look within as they sought the company of their thoughts? Schopenhauer would probably confer that man cannot ignore the "will," his intellect which needs to be nourished; therefore, in a country where the political system limits the material gains of its citizens, the majority of Russians, for example, had no other choice than to explore the frontiers of the mind. Could there be a better escape from the cold reality of the external world than through a game of chess?

Lance could clearly see how schools and television influenced Americans to imitate and conform to the norms of society. Anyone who is different and values other norms outside of the accepted majority within a society is considered an outsider. Although Lance was not an expert on Russian culture and history, he perceived the Russians, at least Kasparov and Karpov, as being thinkers. Thinkers are not passive but very active people, since they normally search out ideas and wrestle to understand them. Like philosophers, they depend on ideas to ponder just as athletes rely on training to prepare their bodies for competition. While playing chess, players are not concerned about ideas, per se, because they are concentrating on all the possible moves they can make with each piece, whether it is a knight, queen, rook, castle, pawn, or king. Furthermore, each player has to counteract the movements of his opponent as well as anticipate his competitor's next move. Thoughts should always precede actions as noted by Plato, the Greek philosopher concerned with defining human logic, because he believed notion were based on experiences or the senses. Once a person has experienced something, he had a foundation for developing an idea. One idea would evolve and bifurcate into many ramifications of thought. For example, when a small child first sees a fire, whether it is in a fireplace or outdoors camping, he becomes enthralled and wishes to learn more about it. He desires to touch it, but once he moves his hand towards the flames, he realizes how hot they are and naturally withdraws. The child quickly learns not to touch a burning flame due to its adverse effects in relation to its magical beauty.

Lance was very interested in the game of chess because one move incited the next one. Accordingly, Schopenhauer recounts how good writers develop and explain one idea before shifting on to the next. The same truth is found in chess because once you have made a move, a player has set the game into motion by delineating a specific course. Without the first play of the game, there would be no subsequent movements. Mankind and, thus, society have learned to value logic, reason, and other forms of thought, since these represent the conceptual foundations of our society and world. When men go astray and establish their own values, society frowns on these individuals as if they were aberrant. In Lance's mind, everything is relative and nothing has to follow any kind of particular order or pattern. Who determines order and who ensconces the "golden rule" for mankind and the rest of humanity to follow?

He continued to muse leaping forward into the future as he recalled eating lunch one afternoon and conversing about an interesting subject with some coworkers from the Texas Legislative Council in Austin, Texas. Silvia, Lance's supervisor, was talking about a lady psychologist who met with them to discuss communication among workers. This lady had put people on the spot by asking questions in regards to their personalities, and she made several accusations based on their answers. For example, one of the participants said she was afraid to assert herself and express her opinions, and the lady accused her of being insecure and immature. Most of the people in the meeting were offended and did not challenge the lady. Lance perceived that many of the things she spoke about were taboo, and most men and women were conditioned by society to hide their feelings of obsession, depression, insecurities, religious beliefs, and other personal convictions.

Lance listened to what everyone was saying. He asked the question: "What is wrong with being insecure or obsessive?" Our psychiatrists and doctors have taught us that these are bad qualities; however, Lance did not consider them as deficient because they were part of the human condition. Schopenhauer claimed that humans complain about the slightest discomforts: an aching toe, upset stomach, and other trite ailments, allowing them to become distraught from the smallest nuisance as if life was supposed to be pain free and perfect. We easily overlook how fortunate we are when we fail to realize things could be worse. As a result, Schopenhauer declares himself to be a pessimist because he accepts suffering as a natural and indispensable quality of existence: no man is free from displeasure and grief. He believes anyone who tries to deny this fact by attempting to live in a world of blissful optimism is a complete fool. Lance postulated the need to view conceptual impressions such as suffering, in an attempt to grasp their deeper meaning, since man cannot ignore ideas due to his rational nature.

Conversely, the psychologist understood the power of conceptions and thoughts and thoughts, which can be used to manipulate people into thinking and accepting certain values and ideals. The clinician, being a thinker, was playing with the group's emotions just like a chess player who moves and manipulates the pieces on the chessboard. In a sense, our schools and society have failed to promulgate and develop thinking individuals who are able to analyze their emotions. Many people are afraid of profound thought because they are forced to face their own reality, which is much easier to evade than confront. By nature, man is indolent, and he must always struggle against the inertia of his mind and body. The television age has added to the caldron of passive viewers who are nullified by the ruminating articulations of others. The body also becomes lethargic because it is easier to eat and remain inactive than to rise into activity by walking, running, or any other physical activity.

Lance realized this discussion with his coworkers was an example of a microscopic problem within the macrocosm of our society. People willingly or unwillingly accept or deny the analysis dispensed by psychiatrists and PhDs without taking the responsibilities on themselves to face their own reality. By looking within, one attempts to answer basic questions: "What is life? What do I believe? How do I find these answers?" People, who do not explore these postulations concerning their lives, will always be dependent on psychoanalyst and therapist to answers these questions for them. These professionals know they cannot solve these enigmas for their patients, yet they can only assist in leading them to pinpoint and confront their own reality. In the end, each person must search for his individual answers.

Karla and Lance spent two weeks in Puerto Rico before returning to Missouri. Karla lived one year with her grandparents in Columbia, Missouri where she completed her senior year at Hickman High School. Lance lived with his aunt and uncle in Kansas City, Missouri. They missed Puerto Rico, but John and Josephine believed it was important for them to spend some time away from home. John knew it was imperative for his children to experience living in the United States, so they would begin to appreciate both cultures.

Lance remembered walking home after playing basketball at the neighborhood basketball court. He missed El Monte, the large apartment complex where they lived. There was a capacious pool there adjoined by a small soccer field. He would never forget the memorable times he swam and played soccer and football with his friends along with the unforgettable and endless evenings he spent in the lobby with his friends: Rawli, Juanesto, Gustavín, Josee, Aimée, Isa, Katrina, Alex, Hilda, and others. They all represented his family. The memories of them sitting around musing, listening to music, and just hanging out together would always comfort him. The ritual of going on a pilgrimage to this "holy ground" around 7:30 every night would impregnate his soulful mind forevermore. The times when Lance and his friends would walk together to the neighborhood theater to watch a movie or pile up in one car and drive to Old San Juan or El Condado, the tourist strip with many hotels, were inerasable from his nostalgic consciousness. The recollection of blowing things out of proportion with the personal effect of laughter from drinking beer and smoking marijuana were tucked away in those corridors of the past. Luckily, those temporally destructive habits were squelched by the love of sports and a more spiritual purpose in living derived from this youthful and experimental foundation.

One night he and his friends were driving to Old San Juan after smoking a few joints, and Lance was sitting in the back seat chortling joyfully. The street lights outside were flashing and glowing iridescently. Rawli and Gustavín were sitting in the front seat, and they looked back at Lance. Lance surreally imagined being in a space ship, and they were asking him where he wanted to go. They were all bundled up in a small light blue Volkswagen feeling its vibration which added to the sensation of taking off into the galaxies. Juanesto, who resembled Mr. Spock, was sitting next to Lance. Everyone's voices, movements, and expressions were distorted and amplified. Everybody was guffawing, and Lance envisioned being part of a psychedelic chimera.

In Old San Juan they stopped at an ice plant and picked up a couple of six packs of beer. Nothing could go wrong. Everything was so majestic and magical that night. They drank and smoked, and they drank and smoked some more. As Lance reminisced and relived this night, he tried to comprehend the fascination most kids have with drinking and smoking pot. The altered state of mind must be appealing, being able to enter into another zone of reality, one not commonly frequented. Lance wasn't trying to escape from any cryptic vexations, since he lived a felicitous family life and got along with his parents. He was just experimenting to see what all the hype was about. It also seemed cool to hang out with the older guys considering they knew things he had yet to learn. Plus, he relished the attention he received from them, as they seemed to be entertained by his propitious and garrulous demeanor. What he soon realized the following morning was the headache and sluggish lethargic apathy that greeted him. This did not commingle well with his athletic inclination and overall well-being.

He also became cognizant that kids are vulnerable to going along with the crowd, as he had done. The emotional excitement of the occasion, which later fades upon reflection, is enticing until one courageously concludes that this is not the desired path to continue trekking. At this junction, one begins to follow the road less travelled, as suggested in Robert Frost's well-known poem; thus, one frees oneself from the traps of the group syndrome where one is most vulnerable.

Lance would never forget the sense of freedom and play he experienced living at El Monte. The pool was the center, the mecca of all the activities during the day. The girls were attracted to Rawli, (nickname Rey del Sol) who had bleach blond hair and a proportionate and well-defined physique. He was very athletic as well as an excellent swimmer. Lance admired and respected him because he was humble and unassuming about his talent. Lance wanted to be like him some day. Rawli, (nickname Rey del Sol) had competed on the Colombian and Puerto Rican National Swim Teams for a number of years; he held several records in the 200-meter butterfly and 400-meter freestyle.

Normally, everyone would hang out at the pool on Saturdays and Sundays. The bright sun was always shinning; the water with its blue and turquoise ripples always careened against the walls of the pool; and the lyrics of Carly Simon, Cat Stevens, the Beatles, Carol King, Eric Clapton, Chicago, the Rolling Stones, and the numerous groups of the '70s filled the air. Lance would always commemorate his friends and the eternal days spent hanging out with them at El Monte.

Chapter 5

KANSAS CITY AND THE CLASSICS

Lance's aunt and uncle, Julie and Derrick, lived on a cul-de-sac in a decorous neighborhood on the outskirts of Kansas City. His cousin Stacey was very charming and demure. She was ten years old, and she had bleached blonde hair. Everyone welcomed Lance to Missouri although he felt some discomposure, since he would be living with them for a year. His room was very commodious and comforting with a blue carpet with gold tips covering the floor. The walls were freshly painted with an off white color which matched the gilded streaks of the rug perfectly. There was a wide window angled geometrically close to the intersecting walls on the right side, which supplied the room with ample light. As Lance blindly stared at the phosphorescence of the resplendent beam of light reflecting from the bedpost, he remembered the words of Arthur Schopenhauer, the 19th century German philosopher: "Money is human happiness in *abstracto*; consequently he who is no longer capable of happiness in *concreto* sets his whole heart on money."

These words from the sagacious Schopenhauer resonated in Lance's mind although their meaning confounded him. Maybe it was because he noticed the affluence of Kansas City and the capacious and grandiose homes, which were lined up symmetrically along State Line, the highway bisecting Missouri from Kansas on the west side of the state. When he considered the poverty, which existed in many of the slum areas of Puerto Rico and Mexico, for example, he began to realize the cruel and divisive realities of the world. A global community governed by power and money, the wealthy versus the poor.

The imaginary state line separated the two. What do Schopenhauer's words truly mean? Happiness is such a difficult concept to comprehend and define. Is it the stillness of the hunter or camper who enjoys and ponders the beauty of the woods; or is it the traveler who admires the ostentatious homes lined up in the distant shadows shaped by oaks, pines, and elms transplanted from their natural environment and transformed into artificial dwellings? These homes must have represented optical illusions to the savage who does not understand the ways of the civilized world. Is this "felicity" in *concreto* or in *abstracto*? These ideas intrigued Lance. The material things of life: the dimensions of his new room, the impeccable color combination of the carpet, the freshly painted ivory walls, and the furniture, which blended, together in such a uniform composition of order, fascinated him. These dimensions, colors, and transfigurations confounded him with great interest and mystery. They comprised aspects of life for him and everyone else. These things could drain man of his emotions and intellect when the acquisitions became all-consuming even if the end product represented happiness in *abstracto*. A sense of well-being was preeminent, knowing one had provided a desirable *shelter* for one's family and self.

It wasn't long before Lance met Timoteo, (nickname Rojo), for his strawberry red hair, who had a long and slender build with his auburn hair lying limply on his head. He had a peculiar bounce in his walk, sort of a hop, which coexisted awkwardly with his laugh. It was a short grunt, which exploded through the air. He was very animated and ambitious with an entrepreneurial drive. When it came to business, Timoteo was very frugal and laborious cutting numerous lawns during the summers in the neighborhood with his lush red *Toro* machine. He always talked about how much money he was making and saving.

The bus that morning was very full as Lance recalled sitting on the edge of a seat three rows from the back. The cold crisp air did not remind him of the tropical weather he was used to in Puerto Rico. He sensed a peculiar aura, as if he were in a dream, with the lambent light of the early morning creeping into the bus; the only audible noise, the cacophonous clamor of brakes and a squeaky door opening and closing, mesmerized everyone on board as they remained frozen in their seats. Shapeless clouds effervesced from everyone's mouths with the chill penetrating their bodies. The frigid sun began to ascend amongst a cluster of leafless trees as it sluggishly climbed through the denuded limbs waiting to be embraced by its solar warmth. The sinister face of winter smiled upon the sun with a mocking glare.

Everything seemed so different at Grandview High School, which was an enormous school compared to the ones Lance attended in San Juan. The building enclosing the classrooms contained many long and spacious corridors. Fortunately, the building was well insulated, and he began to warm-up as he walked through it. At lunchtime he saw the basketball court, which was pulchritudinous with its sheeny oak floors. Returning to his dream state, he envisioned playing on the hardwood, dribbling down court, and jumping up to take a shot. He heard the roaring and deafening crowd in the background. The opposing team had just missed a twenty-foot jump shot, and John, who was a 6'3" forward, grabbed the rebound and passed the ball to Lance. Lance looked up at the scoreboard with only ten seconds remaining in the game and noticed his team was behind by one point. He twisted and weaved with the ball as he dribbled through two defenders. There were seven seconds on the clock as he searched for a teammate, but no one was open. He dexterously cut to the left of his defender leaving him a step behind; suddenly, he was wide open at the top of the key. With three seconds clicking away, he leaped up into the air with a tall opponent positioned perfectly to block his shot; miraculously, he switched the ball over to his left hand in midair releasing it fluidly as it gently slipped through the net. The crowd soared to its feet roaring with astonishment as the buzzer sounded hastily honoring Lance as the hero. In this most ecstatic victorious moment, one he would never forget, the cheerleaders, fans, teammates, and coach all ran onto the floor and picked Lance up over their shoulders.

The bell rang awaking Lance from his glorious dream. His next class was English, and Mrs. Sutter was a young and very attractive teacher. Her shoulder length brunette hair hung freely as she walked unpretentiously in the classroom always expressing her thoughts clearly and energetically. She often wore a short purple dress adorned with white cuffs on its sleeves, which extended to her wrists. He noticed her long fingernails meticulously painted in fuchsia accenting her outfit and persona nicely. Her long eyelashes kept him mesmerized as he had a definite weakness for pretty women, especially when they exuded confidence and self-control. However, his taciturn nature along with being spellbound kept him from really expressing himself in class. Lance always sensed that Mrs. Sutter liked him; it would have probably pleased her if he participated more, yet he was not totally relaxed around the other very opinionated students in the classroom.

Although Lance had fond memories of Mrs. Sutter, he could not recollect any of the books he read in class, nor could he recall any of the class discussions. He vaguely remembered keeping a daily journal in which he recorded some of his personal opinions and ideas. He was sure he probably wrote often about Mrs. Sutter: her sexy ways and those nice snug dresses outlining her slender and curvaceous body. It seemed odd to Lance that a person could spend so much time in school and only think of one or two teachers who were really inspiring. Lance wasn't necessarily invigorated by Mrs. Sutter's teaching techniques even though she exalted a friendly and affable manner, which was unique, since many teachers were indifferent and trite.

He opined that not many teachers read the classics; as a result, their methodology lacked profound substance. When one truly reads and understands this genre, one lives the many lessons promulgated therein. Ernest Hemingway, Dante Alighieri, Ralph Waldo Emerson, Henry David Thoreau, Sor Juana Inés de la Cruz, Saint Teresa of Ávila, and a multitude of others are examples of a macrocosm of writers who wrote and lived their ideas. They provided the fruit for human thought and stirred others to think and correspond freely in a world often suffocated by mainstream society, which stagnates and smothers the creative mind.

Lance could not comprehend why educators and society treated the classics and other great readings as if they were books with ideas, which existed in the past, but which had no relevance in today's world. Today, especially, when the government is trying to reduce the national debt of eighteen trillion dollars, society remains indifferent. When crime has pervaded in the cities across the nation, and when drugs and alcohol have infected the lives of children and many adults, our citizens refuse to engage in meaningful dialogues for solutions. When schools and government spend billions of dollars to solve the educational *apathy*, which predominates in our schools and in the attitudes of our adolescents, administrators place the blame on teachers. Finally, when racial tensions are at an all-time high, primarily between law enforcement officers and Black Americans, earmarked by the August 9, 2014 shooting of Michael Brown, an African-American eighteen year old teenager, by a White police officer in Ferguson, Missouri, we remain clueless in viewing these incidents resulting from a lack of dialogue between divergent ethnic groups to establish harmony not discontent. The Socratic method would help alleviate some of these problems, but our society chooses to ignore the difficult issues. America is composed of individuals looking out for themselves, which is admirable, as long as they don't overlook the collective good.

The classics include the writers who seized the moment to create and recreate. Authors who looked beyond the reality of the present in their attempt to grasp the world of fantasy and the unknown through poetry, the rhythm of words and verses, which uplift the soul, and thought provoking essays among other forms of discourse. In our present day modern society, the absence of true thinkers and creators is due to the significance our society and educational institutions give to rote memorization and stagnant intellectualism. Yes, the federal debt and deficit are problems, which we, as responsible citizens of the United States and the world, must attempt to solve, but men must look beyond the *tentacles* of our materialistic world. Whether our nation pays off the debt and balances the deficit or not, we will still face death at the end of our lives. Let's concern ourselves with life and living.

Moreover, how can people be concerned about life when many are unemployed? The health care system is excessively expensive, and children are not learning, as they should. In addition, the debate concerning whether homosexuals should be allowed to marry legally and serve in the military has consumed our nation along with a multitude of other issues like planned parenthood, for example, an organization accused of selling infant body parts. Should each person become better educated? Does government need a better health care system? Should people spend endless hours debating whether homosexuals should be allowed to serve in the military? Yes, these are essential questions, which must be addressed.

However, a change of philosophy is what we need most. When our definition of life is altered, we can change and solve these problems, or, at least, we can develop a more objective approach to solving them. When we realize jobs, education, and health care are relative matters in comparison to other *drawbacks* in our lives, society can implement revisions and improvements. Man's foremost need is his discernment of who he is and his role in the universe. Primitive man did not depend on health care nor rely on an education to provide him with a better job, so he could buy a house, car, and other luxuries.

Man believes he needs these material items, but in actuality, they are not fundamental for living. Man only needs food, exercise, and a meaning for his existence. He requires time to reflect and walk along nature's path, so he can get to know himself, his Creator, or whomever he believes in. Mankind does not need to manufacture more cars, create more industries, or build more skyscrapers to clutter our cities. Man needs a change of attitude fueled by a new sense of purpose and meaning. Without the deeper probing of ideas, man succumbs only to the capitalistic necessities mentioned above, which are imperative to our lives, but are secondary to the primary significance prompted by classical ruminations.

It wasn't long before Lance met Coach Carmelo, the junior varsity basketball coach. Mr. Carmelo was a tall man whose gaunt shaped face contrasted greatly with his massive feet. His strange physical traits matched his droll personality. His unflattering nature was in sync with his grey sport jacket and blue trousers, which he donned the whole year. He also said the same clichéd phrase everyday: "O.K. boys, I want you to dress up in your gym clothes in five minutes." When Mr. Carmelo switched into his informal attire, he resembled a vulture in human form with his head hanging over his emaciated body and enormous phalanges. He needed a place to belong, and there was no doubt that being a basketball coach and history teacher were his callings. Mr. Carmelo felt like he was sculpting our characters by teaching us the value of discipline and hard work. Our workouts centered around working on a few plays, shooting free throws, and running suicide drills, in which one ran and touched the first line on the court, about five feet from the end of the court; then, one returned to the starting point and ran out and touched the next line, about ten feet out. There were a total of six lines, which he made us run and crotch down to touch consecutively. It was obvious this was his favorite drill in practice because he would like to run us until someone got sick. He gained much pleasure when some kid stopped and regurgitated the transformed hotdog he ate for lunch. Like a vulture waiting and anticipating the undigested food to spill forth in a semisolid and yellowish liquid form, we all sensed that he was salivating during the suicide drills. Lance knew that if he were left alone at this moment, Mr. Carmelo would lap up the disgorged slop without hesitating. Although, now, Lance purposefully embellished this description of his coach with much hyperbole, he would never forget this peculiar and cadaverous man who was consistent though unoriginal.

Lance did not have many pleasant memories of his basketball experience at Grandview High School. He loved the game, but for some strange reason, he felt like he didn't belong as an outsider from Puerto Rico. He reminisced of one game his aunt and uncle attended. He played for five minutes, and he was so self-conscious about every move he made that he wasn't able to execute anything correctly. When he dribbled the ball, it hit his foot and went out of bounds. When he had an opportunity to score a layup, he overplayed the ball and ended up behind the basket. It was definitely a discomforting feeling, one that he would soon like to dismiss. But, such was life and such was Coach Copper, who didn't allow him to play more than a few short intervals, which wasn't long enough to establish any type of rhythm.

Even though Lance did not have a successful basketball season, he did enjoy running cross-country. He would always remember the warmth of the grey sweats and the pair of stripped blue Adidas running shoes, which the coaches had given all the athletes.

Running was so natural, and he soon discovered it to be a thinking man's sport. If you compare running or even swimming to other sports, it is probably one of the few events or the only one in which a person losses himself in thought. When a runner runs ten miles alone in the woods or on a farm road, he becomes one with himself and nature. There is no coach present telling him what to do or how to play the game. The runner faces his own reality and tries to define it. He runs because he is instinctively searching for meaning, and every person wants his life to have a sense of self-worth. Some understand this need consciously, and others intuit this desire subconsciously acknowledging that without substance there is no life worth living.

Henry David Thoreau wrote an interesting book *Walking* in which he describes the desideratum of losing oneself in the woods. Thoreau would periodically go on four-hour walks. He perceived the indispensability of mind and body and the interconnection between them, which provides one's *raison d'être*. In the rustic setting, he discovered the *wildness* or naturalness, which exists in all creatures. The *rawness* we all possess frees us from the prefabricated demands of our modern age. Thoreau went on to say that our legs and bodies were created to walk and exercise so that we could saunter to *la sainte terre*, the *holy land*, on a regular basis. The *holy land* in this context represents the present state of meditative awareness of oneself and his surroundings. When one becomes a walker or runner, one discovers he belongs to the world; the activity of perambulation reminds one of his relationships not just to his job, family, and immediate dwelling, but also to the world. What a concept! Man spends so much time educating himself, so he can eventually obtain decent employment. He acquires money, so he can take away the necessary natural resources for building his home. Once the home is edified and complete, he closes the door to nature, the exterior world, to focus only on the interior aspects of his physical residence. How truly civilized we have become!

Thoreau presents another poignant point in his writings when he states: "When [someone] asked Wordsworth's servant to show him her master's study, she answered: 'Here is his library, but his study is out of doors.'" It's compelling to observe it wasn't just Thoreau who noted the significance of walking and immersing oneself in natural habitats, but many writers, poets, philosophers, and others knew the relevance of perambulating. By exercising, the writer or artist is able to free his mind from the daily concerns, which afflict him, so that he can truly think and create joyfully.

The images of running cross-country would abide with Lance indefinitely. He would never forget running a two mile course in Dripping Springs, a school about 270 miles southeast of Kansas City, Missouri. The rolling hills were pastoral, and the cool smell of fall with its verdant vegetation was invigorating. He would never forget the tranquil *temporal space* before the beginning of the race which seemed to last an eternity. The sun lit up a dirt path traversing the field while its golden drops slowly descended and caressed his face. The other runners stood mesmerized, and a slight nervous and speechless tension permeated the air. The struggle with nature and self was about to commence, one that had baffled men since the inception of time. About a half-mile ahead in the transparent and pristine distance, Lance could see a creek, which weaved itself through the hills. The water slowly trickling down stream, evocative of the constant movement of the ocean with unfurling waves crashing on the crystal pebbled sand of the Caribbean shoreline, was impressed nostalgically on his mind. Water had many forms and shapes just as thoughts emanating from the abyss of man's mind. Lance anticipated the encounter the second before the official fired the starting gun.

The stun of the reverberating sound incited all thirty runners to take off sprinting. They ran down the narrow path leading them through the thicket of a densely wooded area of the course. Lance's thoughts turned inwards as he concentrated on his breathing and his bodily functions. His heart began to pound as it pumped air and blood to the extremities of his legs and arms. The flow of blood, like the flow of water from the creek he quickly approached, encouraged him to continue his solitary battle as he internalized his confrontation with himself, the others he was competing with, and his idyllic surroundings. Instinctively, he knew it wasn't of paramount significance as to who won the race; however, it was imperative to seize the moment by making it vividly real. The vigorous impression of his foot landing heavily upon the tender face of earth was immortalized in his memory as Mother Nature embraced his feet and encouraged him on. The song of the cardinal high above as well as the startling raucous of the woodpecker drilling his beak on the wooden drum of his arboreal friend cheered them on. The image of the setting sun, fading away in the distant horizon, fell gracefully upon the crimson and yellow blanket creating an orange western mask. There alone in nature's grip and with the other runners, Lance grasped for air as he pumped his arms and propelled up the last hill before crossing the finish line and falling to his knees. What an invaluable and memorably intransient sensation! He ruminated and said to himself: "*Cogito ergo sum.*" (I think; therefore, I am.)

Lance walked and reflected pensively as he mused about his existence, which had no meaning by itself without any type of thoughtful deliberation. To exist for the sake of living was devoid of any valid conclusion. Everyone was conceived for a reason, whether it was predetermined or not; thus, it became man's definition of self-metamorphoses throughout his life. It changes much like the seasons of the year brought about from the climate cycles of the earth. Existence resembles the discoloring of leaves in the fall just as a person may modify his perspective on a certain issue. It also exemplifies the bleak and mysterious death, which embraces man in the grey of winter. It is the rejuvenation and excitement that the freshness of spring evokes in man with its red roses, jasmine, and multifarious forms of vegetation engulfing him with its perfumes and aromas. It is the nervous energy of summer, which beckons one to swim in a river, to have picnics in the country, and to travel to foreign lands. It's the transformation, the constant movement, which excited Lance.

Movement appears not only in the plot of a novel, but also in nature when an animal attacks its prey. It is also ascertained in the constant flux of the earth and in the philosopher's fresh ideas, which nourish his soul, intellect, and whole being. Without thoughts his life is devoid of any concrete significance. He who searches for truth knows he may not attain great material wealth; however, he is not concerned with this type of success. He is enthralled by the search feeling a euphoric sense of being when he seeks to understand. The seeker of truth realizes how much he does not know when he embarks on a life dedicated to thinking. He wisely knows that true veracity is found in the inner confines of man's ignorance. For him searching for veracity in spite of not knowing is the hallmark of true knowledge. Precise words, logic, reason, values, and the unknown uncertainties of the world are the tools he uses to chisel away at the meaning of life. The erudite, much like the sculptor, creates his argument based on his perceptions and interactions with his surroundings.

The savant much like the poet is constantly searching for an image from nature, which will refresh and confirm his outlook on life. The poet rides the roller coaster of existence, observing its hardships and subtle beauties. He sees the rose, which blossoms and withers, and he also observes the perpetual movement of the sun rising and setting in twilight circle. The birth of a child, laughter of a mother, tears of death, youth, monotony, academic achievement, and man's failures are valuable images to the poet. Words often escape the poet, and ideas often elude the philosopher when they search for meaning and enlightenment. When the fountains of creativity dry up, it's necessary to lose oneself in nature to recharge the spirit, which is life's engine.

Duke and Lance became good friends. Duke was also on the cross-country team, and he was a fun guy to hang out with. His head was a little larger than the rest of his body. The paleness of his skin contrasted greatly with his freckled face, and his blue eyes sparkled when he spoke with a quick wit revealing his intrinsic love for life. They shared many good times together playing cards during study hall, training, and hanging out on weekends.

During study hall, Duke and Lance would often play cards. Blackjack was their favorite game. Duke would ask Lance: "Hey, Big Dog. Are you chasing any women these days?" Lance just laughed and looked at his cards. "No, I haven't had time. I've been too busy running and playing cards. What else does a Big Dog need?" Duke would tell Lance that they should have played football, since all the pretty girls were interested in the football players. They were the true heroes of the school. Duke and Lance could not figure out why the girls were more attracted to these athletes. Were they more appealing because they were usually bigger guys, or maybe they were more intelligent? Duke and Lance laughed. They felt a little left out, but they really didn't care. They were having fun playing cards and cutting up. Study hall was the only class period during the day when they could really sit back and enjoy themselves.

Lance thought about football, and the big attraction of this sport. He wondered why it was such a popular sport in the United States. People spent countless hours in front of their television sets watching game after game. Obviously, football and sports were essential components of the American culture. Fans enjoyed the contact and excitement of the game. It seemed to arouse an animal instinct within its viewers. Lance believed football represented a virile symbol of male masculinity. Most guys were allured to the physical nature of the game and the sense of overpowering someone. Reciprocally, most women seemed to be captivated by the rugged nature of the men who played the sport.

All countries and cultures seemed to enjoy watching and participating in sports. In Latin America, the popular sport is soccer whereas in Japan and other Oriental countries ping-pong might be more voguish. All men and women, regardless of race or color, are captivated by the challenge and thrill of competing. Competing is a human instinct all men have which they enjoy fulfilling through sports and other activities. Sports, like art or music, represent an art form expressed by the body and mind. When a body is pushed to its limit by the mind, the intellect must listen to its corporal constitution to learn its restrictions. This relationship between the mind and physical being has always existed throughout history; however, many people, athletes and non-athletes alike, do not maintain and nourish this balance.

Desiderius Erasmus, a renowned Dutch Renaissance humanist scholar from the 16th century, understood this relationship between the mind and body establishing a differentiation between the body and soul. The body obviously joins man to his carnal nature; conversely, the soul exemplifies the divine that unites us with God. Erasmus had a great impact on the world of ideological discourse because he was the first to confront the theologians of his times, who postulated that only people capable of understanding the word of God, as presented in the Bible, were the theologians and high priests. The common man did not have the necessary training or the freedom to read the word of God for himself. Erasmus exhorted that all men, whether educated or not, had the right to read God's word. The gospel according to him was intended for all men to come to know God and his holy son Jesus Christ in a personal and individual way. Erasmus was the first to propagate the conviction that men should have the freedom to study the philosophy of Jesus. He rebelled and admonished the churches and institutions where the teachings of God were confined within its walls and interpreted only by their leaders. However, Erasmus insisted in allowing men to learn directly from the life and actions of Jesus so that they might imitate and become more like Him. Erasmus knew God could not be sheltered within the Church, nor could his teachings be safeguarded by the clergymen of the time, just as Jesus prophesized in the New Testament as he preached and challenged the Ephesians and leaders of the Jewish establishment.

The metaphor of God residing in the soul of every man was clearly one Erasmus disseminated during the 16th century. Man by himself needed to worship God on an individual and daily basis so that he could self-examine his own actions and determine whether he was living according to God's will. The attainment of knowledge was ephemeral; therefore, one should devote his time searching for the divine inspiration of God to experience happiness and serenity of mind.

Without contentment and tranquility, man would remain in turmoil with others and himself; thereupon, he would isolate himself from God.

How would Erasmus define the relationship between mind and body as it is depicted through sports in the 21st century? Maybe one can begin to see the interrelationship between history and the development of civilization throughout the ages. Man has always been conscious of corporeal anatomy knowing when he feels pain and pleasure. Throughout the course of time, he has also examined his relationship with the Divine, and in modern day society, he continues to evaluate and examine his alliance with God. He is constrained by his intellect as he evaluates his relationship with God, and as he internalizes by trusting and loving, he suddenly hears God's voice speaking to him.

This desire to commune with God is similar to the quest of the athlete who participates in sports conditioning his body through the will of his mind. His *spiritual mind* controls his body just like the soul directs his thoughts and unconscious mind. The psyche is the force of the athlete, which allows him to develop and express his instinctive desire to compete and struggle. When he challenges himself, he fulfills his need to overcome the *conflict* within. Without this contest, life becomes meaningless for the athlete and culture he is a product of, since it chooses the sport that identifies its heritage. In America football depicts, in a grandiose manner, the embodiment of the athletic pursuit of each player pitting himself against his foe to become the victor, the one who has best trained his mind and body.

Moreover, the violence and contact between football players excite the passions and carnal nature of man. The sport is very vivid with its demonstrative impact of crashing helmets and bodies. This energy is analogous, for example, to the *conquistadores* who discovered and came to the New World. There was a vision in the 15th and 16th centuries by Spain and other European powers to dominate and expand in a New World full of possibilities for profit through the acquisition of gold, land ownership, and fame. This indelible fact cannot be denied, especially, in a vast land like the formative United States, in which pioneers travelled and settled in the West during its early history. The settling of the West characterizes the adventurous and individualistic qualities, which has formed the American spirit and character, one that values and protects its freedom. This inherent temperament is reflected and comes to fruition in the game of football, a metaphoric expression of freedom, power, and exertion defining American society.

Lance deliberated if this individualism was so strong that the American character lacked other qualities, such as the proper development of the intellect. Do Americans as a whole understand the significance of culture, the propagation of music, art, literature, philosophy, and other bodies of knowledge? There is no doubt that in America there were great writers and artists, such as William Faulkner, Mark Twain, Ralph Waldo Emerson, Emily Dickenson, Andy Warhol, Georgia O'Keeffe, Maya Angelou, Langston Hughes, and many others. However, do Americans appreciate and value the ideas and sentiments these authors expressed in their works? Lance often postulated as to whether America's moral and intellectual integrity was impaired and inadequate.

In a nation torn apart by prejudice, violence, drugs and family strife, has America truly searched within to find consolation? In a great nation, which has reveled in the freedom to live and grow within a democracy, are we, as Americans, losing touch with our culture? As a nation of doers defined by progress and ingenuity, are we becoming naive intellectually? Are we keeping abreast with our own morality and that of the world? Do we have the courage to continue walking along the *path less travelled* to find the truth, our salvation from self-destruction and despair?

It's necessary to be doers, but activity without thought is like a barren soil without germinating seeds and nourishing ideas that fuel the growth of the soul. Without the proper pabulum, Americans will fail inevitably and succumb to the ill infestations of society, which corrode our unity as a nation. Adults will continue to raise children, who inherit the indifference of their parents, and foster apathy for learning with no urgency to contribute to the well-being of others within our nation. In a society of doers devoid of cultural enrichment, people will drown themselves in its materialism and selfishness neglecting the lessons of truth, understanding, and sensibility, the pillars that sustain great nations.

Truth is found in the teachings of our families and institutions, many of which are seriously faltering and failing. American schools have not integrated thought and the divergent disciplines sufficiently; therefore, children do not see the interrelationships between disparate forms of knowledge like exercise and math, for example. This dichotomy would have displeased Plato a great deal, since he believed there should be harmony between all things: education, men, politics, and a nation's intellectual well-being. In *The Republic*, Plato stressed the importance of teaching young children gymnastics until they reach the age of ten or twelve years old. After this period, Plato believed the child was ready to study mathematics, science, history, and other formative subjects. By having the children develop and exercise their bodies, they would learn to enjoy good health; hopefully, they would understand that exercise is an activity, which should and can be practiced for the duration of one's life. For Plato the well-being of the corporeal constitution plays such a significant part is everyone's life, since man could not enjoy the *fruits of life* if his health were poor.

Plato, however, understood man could not rely solely on his health alone. He, who spent all of his time exercising and strengthening his body, would limit his capacity to be a complete human being. Acquiring a salubrious physical condition is indispensable, but man's soul and emotional intelligence must not be ignored. Plato intuited that this intangible need of the human spirit could be obtained through music, which should be made available to children in school at a young age to foster their awareness and appreciation of this melodic art form. Music has a way of soothing the conscious and subconscious minds, and its rhythm and harmony are essential components of life. Children learn the interconnectedness between all things including variations in sounds and its association to other forms of expression, whether it is dance, art, politics, or science. There is an underlying coexistence between man and nature, man and self, and people of foreign cultures. With this acknowledgment of music and its significance, the child is now ready to develop his ability to reason being better prepared to study math, science, history, languages, and other disciplines. He is now capable to see the interrelationships between numbers; examine and learn about plants and animals in nature; and thus, assess the impact and meaning of history in his native country as well as in the world at large.

Lance presumed Americans were slowly losing this cultural appraisal, which Plato emphasized. Yes, many Americans exercise to look and feel better because it is the thing to do. But, how many physical education teachers instruct their students to value the relationship between health, music, philosophy, art, and all aspects of society? Plato realized fitness, in this physical and individual sense, was essential, but he also could see its correlation to economics. A nation with a healthy economy can sustain its people when everyone is a participant. If government officials are corrupt and only think of their personal gain, the less fortunate are exploited which weakens the country. Furthermore, if nations like the United States do not speak another language other than English, for example, they will demonstrate clear misunderstandings communicating effectively with Europe and Third World countries in the Middle East, Africa, and Latin America. Most Americans have a microcosmic view of the world because they don't value the relationships between nations, especially those of a foreign language. Our culture does not teach us to seek the unity and intellectual communion among divergent countries as Plato extolled. Lance presupposed the only way men from dissimilar heritages could improve their relationships would be by studying and learning each other's languages. Man can no longer subjugate himself to speaking one language only; thus, Americans and others should consider becoming more multilingual. Only then, as suggested by the Spanish writer José Ortega y Gasset of the early 20th century, man would become a *ciudadano del mundo* (a citizen of the world).

Lance continued to ponder the existing problems in America. The most prevalent one facing America today is the numerous gangs multiplying across the country with the increased violence in American cities like Los Angeles and Chicago. Who should we blame? Should we blame our schools? Should we blame irresponsible parents who neglect and ignore their children? Are our churches and government to blame? Lance believed every segment of society was at fault. There is an abundance of churches across our nation, but why are so many of them segregated? There are still churches divided by railroad tracks and well-delineated suburban parameters where White people live in one area while African-Americans, Hispanics, and other ethnic groups reside in others. Why can't churches of diverse creeds and color get together at least once or twice a year and have a service incorporating elements of worship (songs, sermons, and prayers) representative of every ethnic group participating in a variety of languages, English and Spanish, for example?

Isn't this what Christianity professes? Children and adults become more biased and prejudice in churches lacking a variegation of ethnic diversity. Imagine how magnificent it would be for multifarious congregations to get together annually to have a service in which they include Black hymnals and Anglo music, a bilingual sermon (e.g., English and Spanish), and an international lunch afterwards with a varied composition of music. Why is this so difficult? If children observe their parents interacting with people of divergent ethnic backgrounds, they just might learn how to love one another. Maybe all children will feel like they are part of the fabric that constitutes the United States; thus, this could help them bridge the existing schism with the rest of the world. The inception of gangs rises from the growing need of young adolescents desiring to belong to an American culture that still remains segregated by class and color. As a result, their need for respect, identification, and love emerges and sustains itself in the formation of an *alternative underworld society* of gangs that honors them.

MUSINGS ON ADOLESCENCE

Lance felt strongly about the failure of schools to properly educate and instill young children and teenagers with good values. Teachers are not prepared to address the needs of a wide variety of students from diverse ethnic groups and social classes. In college teachers learn how to write effective behavioral objectives and lesson plans; however, they aren't trained to learn the cultural nuances of minorities. A teacher who does not adopt creative and innovative methodologies will not engage his students; thus, he disassociates himself from them. In addition, Lance knew the old method of lecture and regurgitation was no longer successful in the classroom. Students should be prompted to do activities in which they are encouraged to think and develop their own views. If you don't allow students to extrapolate their own *schematical* designs, they lose a sense of who they are. Without a sense of self-worth and identity, they are more apt to join gangs.

Lance was enjoying his sophomore year hiatus in Kansas City. On Saturdays, he rendezvous with Tim, Kelvin, Chris, John, and some of the other neighborhood boys and play football. He enjoyed bonding with the guys, but he wasn't used to not having *female counterparts* around. That's one thing he really missed about Puerto Rico. Whenever he and the guys would play soccer or basketball at the small playing field next to the pool, there were always gracefully delicate *bellezas* around hanging out at the pool.

John was the comedian of the group. He was always cracking jokes or making fun of Tim, who wasn't the most coordinated person around. Victor was another *hotdog* who drove a souped-up Gremlin. He was always racing around the neighborhood. He was a very gregarious and loquacious Italian-American. Victor was always smiling, and he would always say: "Come on guys. Let's play a game of football."

Timoteo would respond: "No, let's just hang out and listen to some music. Maybe Kelvin has one of those funky joints we can all smoke. Huh, huh!"

Kelvin agreed, "Yeah, let's just hang out and talk man."

John would always get everyone going: "Come on guys. We have the rest of the afternoon to chill and shoot the breeze. Let's enjoy the nice weather and get a little exercise."

Lance didn't mind playing even though he wasn't very excited about football. He preferred playing basketball or just carousing at the local pool with his friends. .

It was easy to compare life in Kansas City with the way things were in Puerto Rico. He was mainly impressed with the commodious homes in Kansas City where it seemed like so many were affluent. Lance thought it was strange to hardly ever see people out in their neighborhoods, since most people worked all the time. When they returned home, they remained inside most of the time. He would often take long bicycle rides on Sundays, and it amazed him that more people weren't outside enjoying the weather.

In Puerto Rico it seemed like everyone was outside all the time, since the tropical weather was conducive for many to spend time outdoors in nature. Lance could rarely remember the days when he was not outside doing something. He was either at the pool, playing basketball, riding a bicycle, bodysurfing, or playing paddleball on the beach. Obviously, the cold weather in Missouri kept people inside for a good part of the year.

However, he would not forget the time he went sleighing behind his aunt and uncle's house. It was a cold dawn resting in the aurora of the day's first light when Timoteo and Kelvin knocked on the door with their sleighs in hand and an extra one for Lance to use. There was an arduous slope in the back of his uncle's house. A creek divided the backyard from the hill and normally dense thicket. The white snow was beautiful, and its softness blended nicely with the disrobed trees which seemed to all be sleeping and draping fluidly on this bleak Saturday morning. The warmth of the sun tried to appear through the sky covered with grey clouds, and the frozen ice in the brook glistened voicelessly as they walked in unison up the hill.

Lance was a little nervous since he had never ridden a sleigh before. "O.K. guys, I'll watch you two first. I hope I don't run into a tree."

Kelvin answered, "It's a piece of cake. All you have to do is steer it like a longhorn Texas bovine with your hands. When you reach the bottom of the hill, try to make a sharp turn to the right so you don't slide into the rivulet."

Timoteo laughed cunningly. "Yeah man, it's easy. Kelvin, I think you should go first since you have more experience."

Timoteo was definitely not a leader. He preferred to follow along. Lance would always remember Timoteo with his ruddy hair and sizable lips. He always pushed his thick auburn hair over to the right side. He had an odd laugh, which was kind of a grunt. He didn't seem too interested in much except talking about girls and making money. Although he wasn't a bad looking guy, he wasn't very outgoing; therefore, he never seemed to have a date. Yet, he was a fun guy to be around. He was always ready to do something, and that's why Lance and Kelvin enjoyed his company.

Kelvin took off down the hill. The conglomerate of frozen white flakes was packed tightly, and the defoliated trees stood staring as he jostled seamlessly through the snow. Kelvin came around the first set of trees and gained speed as he descended the hill. He made a sharp right in front of the iced water hole making it look so easy. Of course, Timoteo and Kelvin were old pros since they had probably been frolicking effortlessly with their toboggan all of their lives. Lance was a little apprehensive since he knew his turn was coming up. Kelvin made it to the bottom and yelled, "Alright."

Timoteo secured his red stocking cap over his head, which contrasted greatly with the white snow. The sleighs disrupted the peacefulness and stillness of the early morning. They were subliminally attracted to this serenity and invigorated by its beauty. A frigid wind blew across the surface of the snow softly touching their faces. The great outdoors was man's constant refuge for thought, play, and relaxation.

For the philosopher, nature represents his library where he searches through the infinite pages of knowledge expressed by the images of birds, the golden brightness of the sun, the silent snowflakes falling on the earth, the transformation of colors and life with leaves changing from dark green to crimson and yellow, and metaphoric droplets dropping from barren branches. He stops to observe, reflect, and learn. The cyclical movement of life is what matters the most, as he concludes: "Media vita in morte sumus." (In the midst of life we are in death.)

Miguel de Unamuno, a Spanish writer from the Spanish Literary Generation of 1898, was concerned about how people avoided the topic of death. Unamuno was influenced by the German philosopher Karl Jaspers who believed a person must understand his demise if he wished to comprehend life. Is death the end or beginning of life? Unamuno was raised as a devout Catholic, and he continued to believe in God throughout his adulthood. However, he disproved of the teachings of the Jesuit and Catholic churches, which did not encourage independent thinking. Unamuno believed each man, by means of his own reflections, should search for the meaning of "human passing". Man must communicate with God through prayer, so the truth can be revealed. No man or institution can tell you what to believe because no one knows for sure what happens after death. Men can only speculate and ruminate about its nature. If it were certain there was everlasting life after life expiration, there would be no mystery or reason for having faith. The afterlife would not be as meaningful; therefore, people might take their lives for granted. Thinking about death helps man to think about his life. If there were not an ending, life would lose its significance. The passing of existence gives purpose to life because we all know our days are counted, and each day man moves closer to his destiny.

Timoteo propelled himself down the hill with leafless trees smiling halfheartedly as he wove in and around each majestic giant. The frozen water of the stream below glistened in the reflection of the sun. Beyond the backwater stood the shadows of homes in multiple colors lost in the fog of profound meditation. Rings of smoke spiraled upwards from their chimneys disappearing in the coldness of the crystalline blue air. Kelvin congratulated Timoteo for successfully completing the run, and they gave each other high fives joining each other in brotherhood becoming one with nature.

Lance prepared himself mentally as he examined and positioned his sled one last time before descending down the hill. Years later he would try to revisit this day, and the laughter he shared with Kelvin and Tim. Sadly, he would find out a decade or so later that Kelvin had died of cancer. *Life is death and death is life.* In his melancholic state, Lance thought about Kelvin's youth and his love for life. Lance knew man lived his life blindly, not knowing what tomorrow will bring. Man constantly evolved and reinvented himself and his existence. Like sled ice sailing contraction circulating around stumps and gigantic leafless elongations of bark from an impressionistic painting, man circumnavigates through the vicissitudes of life with its uncertainties. Lance tried to remember the beige stocking cap over his head, blue gloves, dangling blue jeans, and long brown coat that Kelvin wore. He swirled past the first few saplings without any difficulty, but as he approached the brook he realized he wasn't turning the sled as quickly as he should. Suddenly, he crashed into a tree leaving him out of breath and shocked although he was not badly hurt. He banged up his shoulder a little, but he could tell there were no broken bones. "That was fun guys," Lance retorted, as he began to laugh. Kelvin and Timoteo rushed to make sure he was all right. Once they realized he was not injured, they all sat on their sleds cajoling hysterically and talking.

Friendship was very important to Lance, and he really valued the time he spent with Timoteo and Kelvin. Their conversations were simple centering on girls, cars, money, and past experiences. When they were not sledding, they spent time at Tim's house or Lance uncle's house playing pool in the basement. From time to time, they would go to a movie or listen to music at Kelvin's house. Kelvin dreamed about fixing up a 1967 mustang convertible, which he kept in his garage. It had an immaculate candy red or red flamboyán finish like the *rojo flamboyán* (Puerto Rico's symbolic tree). Kelvin had been working on cars for a few years now, and he was rebuilding the engine of this one. He often anticipated the day he would finally have it all finished, so he could take his babe for a drive in his prized mustang, cruising down a country road listening to Elton John sing, "Goodbye Yellow Brick Road." He could just imagine himself and his woman just strolling through the country, mesmerized by the humming sound of the engine purring silently and efficiently.

It's funny how we all dream about finishing or doing something. We work on a project for so long, and it often seems like we will never finish. Suddenly, the day arrives when we accomplish our goals; however, it always appears like the process and struggle have so much more meaning than the final product. Finishing is important because if there were no rewards, we would not attempt a new project. Nevertheless, dreams and the day-to-day graple of realizing them give meaning to life, and without them we would not live fulfilling lives.

The year Lance spent in Kansas City, Missouri was magical and very memorable, one that he would cherish for the rest of his life. He was thankful for the kindness and hospitality of his aunt and uncle who opened their home to him. He would miss his friends, the panoramic snow, and Mrs. Sutter, his young and voluptuous English teacher. He would never forget Mr. Douglas, his study hall teacher, who wrote in his yearbook: "Never swim in your gas tank, and do not put razor blades in your soup." He never had a real opportunity to get to know him, not having him as a teacher, but for some strange reason, Lance would never forget this quote.

There was a new and recreated freshness in the air as Lance walked along the spewing surf in Puerto Rico. He valued his short sojourn in Missouri, but he truly loved Puerto Rico and the renewing force of the ocean upon his feet. The eternal waves of life erupted on the sand soothing his body and soul. The water and soul were one entity, inseparable by time or space. Lance felt free again with the air and freedom of the vast sea intoxicating him. He truly loved the outdoors, the warmth of the golden deity smiling upon him from the heavens above, and the mass of water surrounding this tropical island (La Perla Caribeña).

Lance did not realize it at the time that the next two years would probably be the most remarkable years of his life. He attended a new high school in *Condado*, a nice residential area bordering the beach. He would never forget Robinson High School. Even though he had attended Spanish public schools for seven years, he was excited about going to a private American school. Lance was definitely more attracted to the American "female persuasion". He wasn't sure why, but it may have been a cultural difference. They were sexier, and they weren't always wearing a school uniform like the girls in the public schools were required to do. It was also possible that Lance, now being a little older, had a new attraction for girls, one he had not fully developed in the public schools. Also, the Puerto Rican girls were more protected by their parents. The American girls were a little more progressive, laid-back, and assertive; they also seemed to have well-rounded personalities and were fun to be around.

Puerto Rico was so different from Kansas City, Missouri because the Missourians, in general, seemed more clannish, whereas in Puerto Rico there appeared to be an openness, which was hard to describe. It was almost as if the weather and nature had a direct effect on people's personalities and demeanors. Everything about Lance's life at this time was hassle free and relaxed. Lance lived with his parents at El Monte, a nice large apartment complex. The condominium was very modern and had two floors with three bedrooms upstairs. His sister Karla had just started college at Baylor University in Waco, Texas. As a reporter for the Associated Press, his father was enthusiastic about his job, and Josephine was a nurse at the Veteran's Hospital. The white walls of his dwelling were very inviting, and from the vestibule one could see the sliding glass door, which opened out onto the porch overlooking a panoramic view of lush green grass and a full-bodied palm tree. The bright sun always filtered cascading through the windows filling the living room with its radiance and clarity. The parlor was simply decorated with a three-chaired-couch made of bamboo with a rusty orange floral design, which matched the golden rug placed on the floor in front of it. There was a chair diagonally across from the couch next to the sliding glass door on the right-hand side. This was his father's favorite chair. He spent countless hours there reading and watching T.V. Lance recalled the rectangular opening in the wall, which separated the kitchen from the dining room. Josephine would serve food through this opening. Inside the kitchen there were two stools with orange seats and chrome legs. The *cocina* was Lance's favorite place second only to his room. He would always sit on a stool facing a counter table, which was built into the wall in front of a set of windows, to eat his breakfast. Turning a handle in a circular motion could open the windows.

Lance played basketball that year at Robinson High School, and normally started as point guard. Coach Sherman usually rotated between

Rufus and Lance at this position. The gymnasium was his place of refuge. Lance and his father, John, used to come to this gym to watch Robinson play San José, two of the best high school basketball teams on the island. The stands would be filled on both ends of the court, and the resounding noise reverberated against the walls. San José usually won, and they normally had a very good coach. It was always exciting to watch a close game. San José was an all-male Catholic school, and most of the fans were guys. Lance remembered the congas and chants they would sing throughout the game: "Todos los de Robinson, todos los de Robinson, son así." They would turn their hands down and claim that everyone who attended Robinson was a *maricón* (homosexual). Lance would never forget Papo Ramirez, a 6'5" center who played for Robinson that year. He would grab the ball with one hand and tower over his opponents. Moreover, he was a very exciting player to watch because he moved very well under the basket with the ability to go right or left equally well.

Now it was Lance's turn to play basketball at Robinson, and his dream had finally become a reality. Practice would usually begin at 4 p.m. every afternoon. Lance was fairly taciturn and usually kept to himself. He knew a few of the players like Maurice, who would be starting as a forward with a good outside jump shot, since they played together in junior high school. Lance also knew Craig. However, Lance didn't socialize much with any of his teammates outside of practice. Before practice began he usually warmed up by taking some outside shots on the side basket of the gymnasium. He always worked on his dribbling, handling the ball well with both hands, and shooting layups with his left hand.

One day while he was practicing, he noticed a girl watching him from the doorway of the gym. She had long blonde hair, and her long slender legs looked good in shorts. Lance had not met many girls, since he was demure and somewhat insecure. He didn't have a car, so it was difficult for him to date. He loved riding his green Raleigh ten-speed to class every morning. It would usually take him about forty-five minutes to get to school. Normally, he would ride down the bus lane, and he always had to pedal hard to keep ahead of the buses. They stopped at many intervals, and this would give Lance time to get ahead of them. The freedom he felt riding his bike was totally exhilarating with the ubiquitous sunlight always shinning and the invigorating fresh morning air filling his lungs.

The oneness he experienced with his bike was the best part of the day, and he loved every minute of it. He felt a certain independence and joy, which he would cherish for the rest of his life. Cars would race by with people stuffed inside while he was free, out in the open air. The palm trees and the constant wind blowing against him causing him to sway were comforting. He rode by the white washed walls of the fences that surrounded the homes in his neighborhood. Red hibiscus flowers hanging over the walls were very picturesque, and the green grass contrasted uniformly with the white and red checkered colors. As he approached the Condado area, he could smell the sea breeze as he freewheeled down a steep hill filling his days with happiness.

Lance was reminded of Karl Theodor Jaspers' book *Way to Wisdom*, the influential 19th-20th century German-Swiss psychiatrist and philosopher. Jaspers discusses the importance of transcendence, which is the ability to think beyond our everyday circumstance here on earth. The philosopher seeks to communicate with God on a daily basis, a never-ending process. He defines the role of the philosopher as being different from the role of the Church. The dogma of the Church has already found the answers to the kingdom of God and how to get there, but the metaphysician never establishes a doctrine about Christianity because he is in constant dialogue with God. He is not intrigued by the definite answers to the riddles of life, but more concerned about the search for truth. He understands that truth cannot be reached by reason alone, and this is why he relies on a constant transcendence in which he communicates regularly with God, the All-knowing. He is interested in the individual's relationship with thought and God, whereas the Church seeks for groups to believe its interpretation of Christianity without further questioning. According to Jaspers, the Church is not interested in dialogue as opposed to the thinker, however, who questions the truths and falsehoods of God for himself.

The thinker considers his own existence, and it is by doubting that he learns to understand himself and his relationship to God. When he deviates from dogma, he is forced to formulate postulations, which stimulate profound thoughts about life. Life for the philosopher is not a system that has been created by institutions, whether it is the Church or government, which he must accept or reject. He is the master of his own life because he frees himself to communicate with God and society without inhibitions. He needs this solitude in which he can escape from the noises and established precepts of a civilized world so that he can reflect and establish his own reality.

Lance was carefree during his junior year at Robinson High School. That afternoon he was dribbling the ball as a child who plays without any worries or concerns for tomorrow. How often do men forget the importance of play? As men grow older, they become overly concerned with their responsibilities and work neglecting to play, which is the counterpart of work. When man "saunters in recreation", he establishes the harmony and balance between himself and nature. Nature is constantly renewing its "youth" and playing as one observes in the seasons: the immaculate flowers begin to blossom in the spring; the birds constantly sing in the summer; the colors of leaves change in the fall; and they glide lifelessly onto the frozen ground in the winter. Abandonment from work and change are synonymous and essential for restoring balance.

The ball bounced off the rim as Lance was distracted again by a striking blonde girl standing at the doorway of the north entrance of the gym. Her figure was dotted like an impressionist painting. He perceived a certain excitement as he noticed her peaceful demeanor, and the calmness attracted him to her. He continued to dribble, as droplets of round raindrops rebounded off the cement floor, pretending not to notice her. She seemed to be a popular girl in school, since she was always talking to someone in a friendly manner, which contrasted with his shyness keeping him from conversing with her.

Coach Sherman blew the whistle, and we all assembled in a circle around him. He had long curly black hair and wore an unkempt mustache. His *bigotito* usually matched his tie, which never coordinated with his shirt or pants. He was very energetic and somewhat of an intellectual because his thoughts always seemed to be miles away. He was short and stocky, and at practice he usually wore a faded blue gym shirt with a zipper down the middle and gray shorts, the polyester type. He also wore a gray and blue dilapidated cap. He was the religion teacher and many of the students liked him, since his classes and lectures were thought provoking. Moreover, he was a good motivator, and he didn't do a bad job coaching even though basketball was not his forte.

Today Coach Sherman wanted us to work on our offensive game, especially against a zone defense (2-1-2). Our first game was against Baldwin High School, and they normally played this type of defensive scheme. Coach Sherman constantly talked about the importance of moving the ball and looking for the open shot. Usually, the offensive setup against a zone was a 1-2-2. Lance was the point guard who would play on top of the key. Maurice, who was the best shooter on the team, would play the forward position with Reggie. Sid and Caésar, (nickname Tubi) would usually play the low post positions taking turns moving to the middle of the key when the ball was on the opposite side of the court. When the low post moved to the center, he created a triangle between himself and the forward and point guard. The three-point configuration set up more options for scoring, and it would sometimes throw off the defense leaving the other low post player open by the basket. Lance liked being point guard, since he handled the ball well and was able to set up shots for everyone else. He was not a top scorer, but he was the best ball handler and passer on the team. Lance and Maurice worked well together because they had the keen ability of anticipating each other's passes and moves.

Lance would never forget the game against Baldwin High School. They had one player who was very good scoring an average of about twenty points a game. He was quick on his feet and handled the ball very well. Before the game Lance and the other players would bang on the lockers as they psyched themselves up for the first quarter. The energy level and emotions were very high, and Lance would never forget the adrenaline rush right before the game. It was kind of nerve-racking for him because he knew the gym would be packed and everyone would be watching. He and the other players wanted to perform well. They ran out onto the court, and the fans and cheerleaders cheered them on. The mystifying girl with blonde hair, who he had noticed all week, was one of the cheerleaders. Lance tried not to think about her as the team warmed up shooting layups.

The contrast between juxtaposed noisy and quiet gym caught Lance's attention. The gym was impressive even though it was not huge. The floor was made out of a very smooth concrete. There were blue and yellow lines, the school colors, which delineated the perimeters of the court. In the center there was a hawk, the school emblem. On the south end of the court there was a stage for school plays and other functions. Tonight the curtains were drawn. The clock and the scoreboard were on the east wall, which was comprised of small concrete blocks containing small rectangular holes in the middle of each one of them. On the west side of the court were the built-in wood bleachers, which were retractable. The baskets hung from the ceiling with transparent backboards. There were two entrances to the gym on the north and south sides of the east wall.

Tonight was a special night for Lance. The bleachers were full, and his parents were there. But, most important of all, the blonde girl, who was a cheerleader, was cheering for him and the other players. This was the moment most people dreamt about: being part of the starting team, playing on your home court with a packed crowd, and the girl you liked the most cheering you on and watching every move you made. This particular evening would linger with him for the entirety of his life, allowing him to revisit it frequently.

The referees blew the whistle and all ten players took their position for the jump ball in the center of the court at the start of the game. Syd tried to out jump his opponent so that his team could gain possession of the ball. Syd tipped the ball to Ned who passed the ball to Lance as he brought the ball down the court. As soon as Lance touched the ball, he was oblivious to the crowd as he focused exclusively on the game. He noticed Maurice cut free under the basket, so he quickly passed the ball to him. Maurice caught the ball, made a fake, which threw his opponent off balance, and scored an easy layup. The crowd roared.

Lance was guarding Miguel, the really good player from Baldwin, who was moving the ball down the court. Miguel was very quick, and it was hard to stay with him because his moves were very deceptive. Lance concentrated on his midsection, since Miguel had some good head, hand, and shoulder fakes. Lance also noticed that defying opponent favored his right hand; therefore, he would drive and penetrate on this side of the court. Lance tried to force him to drive to the left by blocking the opposite side with his body position. When Miguel pivoted and switched the ball to his right hand, Lance tapped it out of his hand and proceeded down the court to score a reverse layup with his left hand. Lance usually shot the ball with his right hand, but John had always stressed the importance of learning how to use the left, especially for protecting the ball when the defender was on the right side. Lance was totally ecstatic after this great play as the gym erupted into a state of pandemonium for the second time.

Lance would look back at his yearbook, and this game would always stick out as the defining moment of his senior basketball year the rest of his life. His team won by ten points, and he scored sixteen, the most he'd ever made in a game. The mental image of Luz, the blonde who watched him practice form a distance, was another defining experience that year. He would always recollect his feelings when he asked her out on a date for the first time during his junior year. He would often see her in the hallway in between classes. It was fourth period, and he was getting his books for his English class. As he turned around he saw Luz standing nearby. He was nervous, but he knew he had to ask her out on a date. Lance looked at her and said, "How are you doing today?" Luz responded, "So, so. I think I just bombed my biology exam." Simultaneously, as the bell rang, he blurted out: "Would you like to see a movie with me this weekend?" Luz's eyes sparkled and without a moment's hesitation she said, "I would love to." Lance was so relieved she would go out with him. He told her he would get her phone number after school. Lance went to his English class in a state of euphoria with a huge load lifted from his shoulders. He felt an excitement he had never known before in his short lifetime. Everything seemed so perfect, so right.

Lance thought about Augusto Pérez, the protagonist from the novel *Niebla* by Miguel de Unamuno, the well-known Spanish 20th century writer. Augusto was looking for a woman to marry, the only relationship lacking in his life. He fell in love with Eugenia; however, she loved her boyfriend Miguel who was a bum. Miguel did not work, and Eugenia needed money to pay the mortgage on her house. Consequently, she decided to accept Augusto's offer to wed her, since he was very affluent. He gave Eugenia a large sum of money, so she could prepare for the wedding. Instead of using it to pay for her white-astonished gown, flower arrangements, and other necessities, she took the money and eloped with Marvino, leaving Augusto brokenhearted and depressed. Augusto was aghast not believing this was happening to him. He had everything he ever wanted except for love, a void he could not fill in his life. Being superstitious, he blamed God for his misfortune and unhappiness, since he had been a faithful Christian all of his life knowing he deserved better than this.

Unamuno expresses his religious doubts through Augusto's character. He had been a devout Catholic all of his life, but suddenly, he began to doubt the existence of God after his wife had given birth to a deformed child. He could not comprehend why this happened to them; as he grew older, he was perplexed by the thought of death. "Why couldn't all humans be immortal? Wasn't God immune to death?" Unamuno created Augusto, and the author speaks to him as if he were God. Augusto represents man who listens to God. He uses this abutment because Unamuno desperately wants to communicate with his Creator; however, he is tired of depending on his faith. Unamuno had been raised as an unwavering Catholic, who did not question the beliefs of the Church, because one was supposed to accept its tenets without ever doubting its truths.

Love and the understanding of God were very relevant concepts in Lance's life, which he wanted to define and comprehend. At that exact moment, the bell rang. He felt a strong passion and desire in his heart when he asked Luz out on their first date. He discovered something within himself, which he had never known before. He wondered about the multitude of people who had lived their whole lives without ever falling in love. Even though love seemed so enigmatic, he felt a certain joy, which was new to him.

That afternoon Lance rode his bicycle home after basketball practice, and he was very relaxed abounding in the security of his new found self-confidence. He was also a little apprehensive because he could only think about his date on Saturday night. He speculated about what he would wear and how he would act. Would he say the right things? Would they have enough in common? Without dwelling too much on the future, nevertheless, he tried to revel in the moment of solitude as he pedaled home. He savored the soft breeze blowing through his hair and the cozy warmth of the late afternoon sun.

There were so many uncertainties in life adding to its vicissitudes. A person could never be certain of anything because things continually changed and never remained the same. The only exploit that does not transform is our past; however, the present and future evolve continually. Lance was hopeful about his date with Luz sensing this was a turning point in his teenage repertoire.

Lance spent the morning washing his parent's white Ford Pinto. He dressed himself with a nice pair of slacks and a fitted shirt an hour early; then, he sat down in the living room with John and watched part of a basketball game on T.V. In those youthful years, Lance always dreamt of playing professional basketball someday. The players were so graceful, and they moved so effortlessly. John was an eternal optimist who had always encouraged him to consider playing college and possibly salaried ball later on. Lance was never big enough nor that good to play college or professional ball. However, this never stopped him from aspiring to become a great player.

At 5:30 p.m. Lance got into his parent's car and drove to Punta Las Marías, the residential neighborhood where Luz lived. As he drove through the parking lot of El Monte, the large apartment complex where his family resided, he noticed the lush palm trees blowing in the wind. It was a clear sunny day, and the freshness of the afternoon invigorated him. He drove through Baldrich, a plush neighborhood, which he knew intimately. He could not count the numerous times he walked through this part of town with his father as they went to play basketball at a nearby court, or the many times he and his friends walked to the local movie theater. Afterwards, they would eat ice cream at Taste Freeze. This familiar sight kept him company as he approached Highway Las Américas, which would take him to Luz's house. He was excited but also a little anxious at the same time.

The last image that came to his mind before he entered the ramp to the highway was one of him dribbling up and down the court at Baldrich. The court was barren and isolated, and at 5:45 p.m. there was no one there. The closest facility was a tennis court on the east side and Osuna High School on the west. School was out, and all the students had gone home. The baskets never had any nets, since they were probably stolen a long time ago. The sun was usually beating down on the court's cement, and Lance could feel the heat penetrating his converse tennis shoes as he weaved diagonally from side to side and up and down the hot surface. He would twist effortlessly straight ahead with the "round cowhide" and then pivoted to his left then, he would go to the opposite side of the court and turn to his right. Sweat dripped profusely from his brow, and an erratic cool breeze would comfort him sparingly. Lance relished the solitude in which he perfected the skill of handling a basketball with both hands. This was his escape where he spent multitudinous hours alone practicing, searching for meaning. He wanted to understand his love for the game. At the time, he did not realize he was learning how to depend on himself and to become independent. He realized in his quiet reflections that happiness was the end result of hard work and persistence.

Chapter 7

FINAL INTROSPECTIONS

Lance was reminded of the 19th century German philosopher Friedrich Nietzsche's eternal reoccurrence where he believed life repeated itself continuously. The seasons changed each year, men were born and died, and the sun rose every morning in the east setting in the west. Lance thought of the image of a tree, which is cut down. The wood is used to build a home, desk, or piece of furniture, which is engulfed by flames in a fire. The ashes are the nutrients nourishing the earth, and from the earth the seed grows into another tree. This cycle repeats itself over and over again. Man is bound to this cycle, one he cannot escape from but can learn to live within it. Nietzsche does not clarify what happens after death? This is a difficult question to answer because no man has died and returned to earth to discuss life after death. The exception would be Jesus who died, was resurrected, and went on to heaven to live with his Father. Man can only speculate as to what awaits him after death. If life after Jesus' demise were not a mystery, philosophy and the world of ideas would probably not exist because men would probably understand everything. The truth of life would be at man's immediate disposal, and there would be no need to search for meaning.

Lance's routine on the basketball court was a ritual he performed on a daily basis. Subconsciously, he was struggling to understand his purpose in the universe. He sensed it was necessary to practice to perfect his skills just as a philosopher must allow the *gray matter* of his brain to dance freely. Lance knew it was incumbent to train because it was meaningful to him. Man is different from animals and plants, and he is perplexed by his ability to think and reason. The solitary cat wonders aimlessly through life, dependent upon the stimulus of the environment around him. Its instinct to catch a bird or mouse is natural, and it's not something it ponders and chooses to pontificate its meaning. The kitten's willingness to play and explore is not an activity it consciously wills to do. The philodendron remains motionless to the human eye as it gradually stretches and grows in search for light. It doesn't meditate on its ability to photosynthesize. It doesn't observe man's peculiar nature, since it exists independently of him. The flora and fauna are part of the vast universe. Although they do not have the ability to think, they are elements that stimulate thought in man. Without the plant and animal kingdom, man would probably not develop his reason and logic because the world would be devoid of things to classify and study. We owe our thanks to Aristotle who made many advances in the study of nature and philosophy in the ancient world.

The palms of Lance's hands were sweaty when he put the Ford Pinto into park in front of Luz's house. Luz had invited her friend Michelle, who was also going to the movies with them, and who would later spend the night with Luz. A seven-foot fence surrounded the front of the house. Luz came to the gate as soon as she heard Lance pull up. She wore Levi jeans, a white blouse, and Dr. Scholl sandals with her long blonde hair blowing freely in the breeze. "Hi, Lance, how are you?" Lance was a little nervous. "Hi, you look great tonight!" Luz blushed as she coyly replied, "Thank you. Why don't you come in so you can meet Michelle and my mother?" Lance took a deep breath, since he certainly hoped Luz's mother would approve of him.

Marisol, Luz's mother, was a very warm and personable lady. She was about sixty years old with bleached blonde hair and a dark tan. She was a very attractive lady and smiled often. Lance liked her immediately, and she seemed to like him as well. She asked him if he would like something to drink. Lance replied, "No ma'am, I'm fine." They chatted about school and sports. Michelle and Luz were both cheerleaders. Marisol asked Lance: "How long have you been playing basketball? Luz tells me you are really good." Lance responded: "Oh, I've been playing for about six years. I started playing when I was about nine years old." The house was simple, but very quaint and clean. A soft pastel color blended in nicely with a two-toned couch placed under a painting of Marcel Duchamp's *Nude Descending a Staircase*. It was a small house with two bedrooms and a bathroom; the dining and living rooms were adjacent to each other with a small kitchen in the back. Luz lived close to the beach where a continuous soft zephyr filtered through the open windows.

It was 7 p.m., and they were going to see the movie *Earthquake*, starring Charlton Heston, which started at 7:30. In the car Luz and Michelle talked about the next basketball game. They were excited because the team was going to take a road trip to Ramey Air Force Base in Aguadilla, about sixty miles west of San Juan. They also "prattled" about their classes. Lance was a junior, and Luz and Michelle were both sophomores. "Sra. Martínez is a nice lady, but she sure is monotonous. I have a hard time staying awake in her class," Lance observed. Luz added: "Wait until you take Mr. Valenzuela for junior history. He never stops blathering, and you are supposed to take notes the whole class period." Although Luz was a sophomore, she was taking an advanced history class, since she was an honor's student.

They arrived to the movie theater, and Lance paid for the tickets even though Luz and Michelle insisted on buying their own. The theater was packed, but fortunately they were able to find three empty seats towards the back. Lance sat on Luz's right-hand side, and Michelle sat next to Luz. It was difficult for him to concentrate on the movie, since he was so nervous. He kept thinking about making a move on Luz.

He always thought it was necessary to show a girl you liked her by trying to kiss her during the movie. First, he placed his arm around the back of her seat barely touching her shoulder. Luz pretended not to notice the advancements, but they were obvious. He didn't feel comfortable, but he was compelled to try to kiss her. About midway through the movie, he leaned over and made an attempt, but she never turned her head. It was obvious this was neither the right time nor place. He blushed, but luckily, they were in a dark theater, and no one noticed.

Lance's mind wondered as he thought about all the kids in the world, and the experiences they had during their first date. His thoughts drifted to the war in Bosnia, a country torn apart by fighting between Muslims, Serbs, Croatians, and the Herzegovina people in the spring, 1993. Basically, these ethnic groups had been at odds with each other since the 13th century. The war broke out again when Croatia and Slovenia seceded from Yugoslavia in 1991. Although Lance did not comprehend or have the knowledge to understand the conflicts in that part of the world, he was confounded by war. As he looked at a picture from the *Dallas Morning News* of a woman with a dark scarf over her head holding the cranium of a dead person, someone very close to her, possibly her husband, son, brother, or sister, the anguish and pain she felt were self-evident. People in this country suffered in a way that was difficult for Lance to comprehend. These people did not have the luxury of buying a new car or home. Nor did they have the opportunity to get an education or a good job. He thought about the thousands of kids his age who were dying and not able to experience their first date and kiss.

He was concerned about the situation in Bosnia. Somehow he wished he could help, but he didn't know how. He didn't know if he should feel guilty or not about the thousands of people perishing in Bosnia. After all, it wasn't his country or problem. These issues were difficult to address, and he wondered if there were any answers to these inquiries. He thought, for a moment, about Voltaire, the 18th century French writer and philosopher who wrote Candide, a novel in which he depicts an evil and inhospitable world. Voltaire suggests that God cannot possibly love the people of this world because he permits men and women to hate and kill one another; he allows greed and racism to exist. God basically permits evil to exist in the world.

Voltaire, Jean-Jacques Rousseau, Denis Diderot, and other French writers were concerned about these issues, which separate men. Voltaire asked himself, "If God were a caring God, why did he allow his son Jesus Christ to be crucified on the cross?" He did not understand this kind of love. Lance read voraciously because he wanted to learn more about the classics and what writers had to say about moral questions: the issue of good and evil, man's struggle to understand his own self, and other topics. He speculated whether it was morally correct for him to be concerned about these issues. Why should he care about the situation in Bosnia because it did not affect his life? It was depressing to think about, since he had his own afflictions to contemplate and solve. He lived in the "I come first age" in which everyone was expected to drown in his own narcissism.

Plato also stressed the importance of a moral and uplifting education. He criticized the arts during his time because many plays were not morally edifying. He believed plays, poetry, and music should entertain and educate. Many of the plays, poems, and music compositions during the Greek period were not appropriate for children. The arts were lewd and vulgar much like a considerable portion of the *pop art* today. Plato opposed this type of art because it did not teach; it did not represent the classics, which are invaluable because the penmen wrote about heroes and universal themes, such as love, war, peace, integrity, and justice. These poems, songs, and stories were well-written, and they were meant to inspire, entertain, and develop the moral qualities of man.

Lance was committed to learning and comprehending the problems afflicting mankind. He believed it was necessary to be constantly placed in someone else's shoes to acquire compassion for another perspective. He knew he couldn't solve the conflicts of the world, but at least he could educate himself so that maybe he could inform and share his opinions with others. Maybe after a long period of time, people could begin to dialogue and respect each other's perceptions. Lance firmly believed people must become educated, not to separate themselves from the world, but to realize they are all part of the same community. As people begin to adopt this mentality, they can engage in a universal dialogue, one that is continuous because the difficulties of the world are multifarious. With a sound education in the arts, mathematics, and philosophy, people can acquire the foundation for creative thinking. This would purge men of the senseless prejudice, greed, and hate, which grow and fester in the minds of less educated and suppressed individuals. Without this overhaul in education, men will continue to live in their own isolated chambers. As a result, there will be no need to communicate with others, since men will eventually destroy each other and their global civilizations.

That night was a memorable evening. As Lance drove home with Luz and Michelle from the movie theater, the ocean resounded in the sunken corridors of his subconsciousness. The moon illuminated the road as he fumbled for the right words to say. The outside world seemed to be watching him as he drove into the silent wake of the night's soothing embrace. The soft breeze of the sea engulfed his spirit as he tried to remember that evening tucked away in the recesses of his mind, a perplexing circumstance. Man created an *aberration* in time, which he originally meant to control; yet somehow it mystified him. Time is the unrelenting abstraction, which classifies periods into days, weeks, months, years, decades, and centuries. What would life be without time? Would man be lost?

Man wouldn't know when he should go to work, when to sleep, to eat, and to wake up. There would be no order to his life, and everyone would be disoriented without deadlines to meet. He would drift through life without being cognizant of the day or year. He would have no measurable control over his life and the lives of others. Why does man have this inherent need to dominate and subdue?

Maybe man needs to learn how to let go, to decontrol. He must allow himself to imagine his life without the constraints of time. If he neglects to challenge the established beliefs and concepts of modern cultures, he cannot elevate himself beyond the boundaries created by society. Man should learn how to question and recreate ideas accepted and followed by nations, not so he might become radicalized, but so he can become a thinking individual. Often man recites the ideology of the great thinkers and writers like Plato, Jean-Jacques Rousseau, Francis Bacon, John Locke, and Immanuel Kant, for example; however, he does not use the thoughts of these great thinkers as a foundation for internalizing and formulating his own outlook on life and the world. Our educational systems throughout the world stress the importance of studying the classics, but they rarely encourage students to devise their own creed about spiritual or political matters, for example. Not only should schools teach students about the classics, but they should also encourage them to become "modernists." Students should be inspired to question, think, and reexamine the beliefs, traditions, and established ideas of today's society as well as of the older cultures of the past. This type of education will allow people to view the complexity of the world from a vantage point in which they realize there are no quick solutions to poverty, hunger, wars, prejudice, and injustice. One will acknowledge there are a multitude of mindsets regarding these issues. Henceforth, this multifarious and global nature of man should not inhibit and cause him to build barriers of miscommunication; however, this divergent quality should be cherished and desired by all people. Once it is accepted and valued, people of the world can begin to see each other as one entity in which everyone participates and corresponds to the whole. Each person's contribution gives him a purpose and identification from within to share so that he can live peacefully with others, and history can advise him of past mistakes to maintain this harmony between nations.

 Lance thought about Miguel de Unamuno's thoughts regarding la *nivola*, a word he created to redefine la "novela" or novel. Unamuno wrote *Niebla*, which is a novel he creates, not with a planned storyline, but with a spontaneous flow of thoughts and events. His *nivola* is not predetermined, but is determined as his thoughts are expressed through his pen without guidelines or limitations. He believes it should be created by the act of writing and thinking exclusively. This type of writing, as defined by Unamuno, is the thought, which nourishes the soul because the author frees himself from the constraints and rules governing the process of writing a story according to the parameters set by "good writers." Developing the character, plot, climax, and conclusion are not important. Ignoring these restrictions are necessary for creating the *nivola*, a total abstraction and redefinition of the traditional novel.

This type of creative freedom was exciting because it would never limit or restrict Lance from trying to understand the complexities of the world. He was disappointed with the universities, such as Harvard, Yale, The University of Texas, Stanford, and many others, which were overly concerned with prestige and power rather than a firm commitment to education, especially for their students. Lance was disenchanted because in a way academia had corrupted the minds of men. He would no longer trust institutions, which would often hide behind a veil of pretension. Lance only saw an academic *monster* with an insatiable desire for recognition and fame, which could be depicted in the infamous painting *Saturn Devouring His Son* by Francisco José de Goya y Lucientes, the late 18th and early 19th centuries well-known Spanish artist. Society is brainwashed by institutions, which coerce Americans to believe that a diploma from one of these respected universities will guarantee success, respect, and prestige. These academic establishments are failing to educate students because their priorities have become confused, not in the struggle for understanding the truth but in gaining power. The great universities are not inculcating their pupils with the value of thought, but they are promoting the value of materialism, power, fame, and corruption.

The American people are bewildered by the problems its young adults face in the 21st century. They are the victims of the *malfeasance* of higher education, which hides behind the pillars of research and publishing as they fail to educate. Of what value is a book to man if he is not motivated to read and learn for the sake of learning? The problem confronting our nation is that we do not explore the value of reading. Yes, we spend billions of dollars on programs and centers for helping the illiterate. However, we should teach our children and people the implications of thought by understanding that art, for example, is an expression, which liberates man from his condition here on earth. Music is a means to express our deepest emotions and sentiments; philosophy is a medium by which man can assess and evaluate ideas from the past. With this in mind, he can conceive his own "cogitations" as he learns to respect those of others. When a man thinks, he *becomes* and begins to exist. When a person truly lives, he seeks knowledge not to improve himself so that he can oppress and suppress others, but so he can understand his life.

The world has finally witnessed the Fall of Communism depicted visibly with the destruction of the Berlin Wall in 1989. But, doesn't communism still exist in our government and institutions today? Man still struggles against the corruption and power of our democratic nation where the bourgeoisie and proletarian are still alienated from one another. Karl Marx, the 19th century Germany social scientist and revolutionary, was correct when he affirmed this struggle would continue indefinitely. One can only hope that men will come to their senses, especially, if they have had the leisure to study and reflect upon life. Unfortunately, many have used their talents and knowledge to inflate their egos and become more narcissistic. Egotism, like the violence depicted in the painting *Saturn Devouring His Son*, destroys and alienates men and countries. How sad it is to seek and gain the power of intellectual thought, which often becomes the *poison* that kills the continuous dialogue between students, professors, government officials, citizens, and people of the world.

Lance believed that, in many instances, students should become the educators because their innocence and idealism are pure. Their search for knowledge and understanding had not become tainted with the *blood* of power and fame. Incorruptibility is the key for human understanding. A child loses his innocence through the course of his life when confronted with the realities and hardships of existence. He realizes living is not just a promenade through the park of an eternal spring. He comes to apprehend the struggle all men experience: the constant battle with self, nature, and others. Nevertheless, when he searches to recognize his condition and environment, he unveils the truth and regains his innocence when he willfully chooses to do so. Man must learn to regain his *pure state* if he wishes to live in unanimity with himself and others.

Becoming nostalgic again, Lance reminisced about a class he took with Mr. Brown, his religion teacher and basketball coach, during his senior year at Robinson High School in San Juan, Puerto Rico. He could picture Coach Sherman's thick black eyebrows forming a bridge across his forehead. The polka dotted tie and polyester jacket always amused Lance even though the attire contrasted with the seriousness of class discussions. His curly black hair with streaks of grey matched the blackboard on which he wrote the word "morality" with white chalk. Yes, this was the theme of our discussion that day. Lance gazed through the windowpane of the class as he searched intuitively for his definition of morality. The meaning of life was so simple yet so complex. Life seemed so transparent at times; however, it was always distorted and obfuscated in other occasions. Why? Lance could not comprehend life's mysterious incongruities, but he insisted on musing upon them. Would he ever understand?

Sentimentally recalling his senior class trip to Jobos, a popular beach area on the northwestern coast of the island, Lance lost himself in the past. There were about sixty people in his class, and they rented ten cabins. It was a breathtaking weekend with a brilliant sun and steady air pockets stirring up impressive waves. Juan, Manuel, Ray, and Lance commuted in the same car driven by Ray's uncanny ability to pass cars as we listened to the tunes of Eric Clapton, Grateful Dead, and Joe Cocker. We were young and impetuous guys guided by our leader Ray, the master of our fate who exuded a sense of calmness and confidence, getting us to our destination quickly. Juan had bleach blond hair, and he was Ray's counterpart, shy and quiet, but with a good sense of humor. We would always kid him by saying, "Hey Petey, let's get where we ain't." Manuel was the athlete of the group, lean and muscular. He was the starting quarterback of the football team, captain of the baseball team, and lead sprinter running the 100 and 200-meter dashes on the track team. He had talent but sometimes lacked discipline, since his new fondness of girls, who were attracted to him, became a distraction. Actually, girls became a diversion to all of the guys. Lance was just another dude hanging out with the boys, often insecure and demure with a keen ability to cover up his self-doubt. Instinctively, they all realized they were transforming from adolescence to young adults, and the class trip was representative of their rite of passage.

They finally arrived to the beach resort at Jobos. The plethora of palm trees danced rhythmically to the beat of the wind with the calm and angry force of the sea resounding on the sand. There was such an impetus, a wild and vivid energy in the sea personifying strength. Yet, there was also a feeling of imperturbability about the ocean, which was mystifying. The mellifluous sound soothed Lance as they unpacked the car. The soft sand embraced his toes as he carried his small night bag in one hand and tucked a case of beer under his right arm. They were definitely going to do some partying. Why was *la fiesta* (party) another component of the rite of passage for the adolescent and teenage experience?

Retrospectively, Lance looked back now at those years lost in the past, but frozen forever within the corridors of his mind. *La fête* (party) must be the ceremony of freedom, defiance, and self-liberation. What do teenagers deride? Lance searched within as he tried to comprehend the principles behind this belief. John Locke, the 17th century English philosopher and physician, wrote a very interesting book *Of the Conduct of the Understanding*, which changed the way many savants and educators view their understandings of themselves and the world. Locke affirmed it was important to examine the self to determine the principles, which lead a person to form a conviction or belief. Is the concept of "partying" a conviction or postulation? It probably is neither. Is it a habit? Yes, it probably is. It's possible it's a proclivity, which has been passed down from one generation to the next. Not only is it a disposition predominant among adolescents, but it also defines the status quo for many crossing the line into adulthood.

El festejo (act of carousing) being the counterpart of work and study is a social behavior. However, why are drinking alcohol and smoking pot two important activities for "true" partiers? Can't teenagers and adults alike socialize and have a party without these two components. Yes, they probably could, but obviously, marijuana, which is now legal in many states, such as Colorado, along with alcohol are attractive to teenagers because of the prohibitive laws regarding minors. Parents and society are undoubtedly concerned about the adverse effects of these intoxicating substances on teenagers or any person, since they are sedatives, which could lead to many tragic accidents while driving or could be a springboard to more addictive drugs like cocaine and heroin.

Upon examination, Lance knew he did not have the answers or solutions to these probing questions, which have bewildered many over the years. Nevertheless, it was imperative to ruminate and ponder them so one does not subjugate himself mindlessly to these societal rituals as many do, which in many cases destroys lives and relationships between families, spouses, and friends. Lance concluded each person should constantly search for the truth, not necessarily the *veracity* of the world, but one's own personal authenticity.

Manuel and Lance quickly changed into their swimsuits. Lance always discerned a calling when he arrived to the seashore. There was a swell of waves crashing about half a mile away from the shore. From the distance standing by the littoral cabins, they did not seem ominous, since the sets were coming in parallel to a large rock formation. The rocks formed a perfect barrier for the entourage of water to develop, since this beach area was located on the northwestern seaboard of Puerto Rico, which aligned perfectly with the trade winds that blew in from the northeast. Manuel and Lance returned to their cabins and picked up their fins. They decided they would climb the rock and jump into the area where the waves were breaking. Maurice, the star of the varsity basketball team, decided he would join them. Manuel and Lance kidded him because bodysurfing was definitely not his sport, but nevertheless, he had a competitive spirit and was ready to take on the challenge. Maurice was slender, agile, and tall, which was appropriate for a basketball player. However, it was doubtful he could withstand the force of the perfidious ocean. Manuel and Lance were more compact and muscular, since they had been swimmers most of their lives. Even as experienced swimmers, they instinctively were cognizant of the risk due to the size of the waves, the strong current, and distance from the shore. The spume of the porous matter and air soaked their feet as they stood on the edge of the rock.

The wind blew stronger as the waves crested uniformly above the surface of the sea. The majestic waves looked monstrous now that they were closer to them, and they glided evenly and powerfully on the water. Their force seemed endless in the mild heat of the late afternoon. In the horizon the sun descended into oblivion engulfing its crimson and scarlet robe bedazzling them with nature's continuous movement. Without this cycle man would be lost lacking the ability to reason logically because everything would be in a constant state of chaos. God through nature provides a rhythm and structure in the world, which are necessary for ensconcing a rational life founded on faith. Without this natural motion and change, there would be no order. The cyclical rising and setting of the sun impart a backdrop for man to observe his surroundings; thus, he becomes aware of his significance allowing him to recreate and invent itself. Lance stared into the sea realizing it was anomalous for man not to see and unveil the essence of nature's greatness. He shivered as he looked at Manuel and Maurice, and yelled, "Let's do it."

Without further deliberation, all three of them dove into the water from the large rock compilation, since the strong current inhibited them from swimming from the beach to where the waves were breaking. Once they were immersed in the water, they realized the treacherous conditions, since there was an undercurrent pulling them into the wake of the mammoth formations. Nevertheless, the freshness of the water was invigorating. When they came up for air after sinking from diving into the sea's mouth, a colossal wave was fiercely advancing towards them. It was phenomenally huge, and one's perception of size is always different once in the grips of the formless presence. Lance could feel the hair rise on the back of his neck as the voracious mass of water thundered forward beginning to break, meaning the crest of the wave had peaked; it was rolling forward, which was not ideal for riding. Lance and Manuel knew they must swim under it to avoid getting caught in the middle of its wake where all of its force is generated. Lance took a deep breath and went under. He could feel the roaring force as he submerged himself beneath its ominous violence, spiraling and contorting his body as it whipped him around. It seemed like he struggled underwater for a minimum of five minutes as he tried to swim to the surface to get a new breath of air. When he finally surfaced, another huge wave came barreling forward. There was no time to think as he took another deep breath and dove below the massive body of water. He did not see Manuel or Maurice, and he wondered if they were all right. Sensing this wave was stronger than the first one, there was no doubt in his mind that it was at least ten feet high. He only thought about making it to the surface, since the water mass had pushed him deeper into its fearful and dark abyss. The dense spume slowed him down as he desperately toiled to make it to the top. He eventually surfaced to grasp that miraculous lifesaving inhalation of air.

Another gigantic wave was approaching rapidly, but this time Lance had enough time to catch it. He swam towards the wave as it began to swell and caught it in the middle of its voluminous mass propelling him forward. He would enjoy an awesome ride that lasted for several minutes. He knew this was a magnanimous force he had never experienced before. The wave was breaking to the right; therefore, he stretched his right arm out 90 degrees, which functioned as a rudder, allowing him to ride in its tube. In a state of complete exhilaration, the crystal blue mass splashed over his head forming a geometrical cylinder as he was jetted through its epicenter in a perfect state of coexistence. Lance would never forget this feeling of awe, wonder, fear, and exuberance as he was delivered from the "vise grip clamps of death" to the sweetness of life. From this day forward, he would have great reverence for the powers of God, Nature, and the *Frailness of Existence*. The impetus of the wave diminished within two hundred yards from the shoreline where he could see the friendly smiles of Manuel and Maurice waiting for him. The triumphant joy of making it to *tierra firme* (firm land) with his friends was everlasting.

Riding that wave represented a turning point in Lance's life. He had wondered about nature before, but never had he experienced the magnitude of its ominous force like this. It invaded man's daily life sometimes manifesting itself sinisterly in the form of a tornado, earthquake, tsunami, or forest fire. Many people seemed oblivious to its power, especially, when it takes the form of a soft breeze in the early morn blowing gently through an open window with the graceful rising of the sun and songs of cardinals and other multitudinous birds filling the air. Those blissful mornings commemorated the days when Lance would ride his bike to school during his junior and senior years at Robinson. He would often try to recall rolling down the long exterior hallway of the second floor of El Monte Apartments where he used to live. His green and black ten-speed Raleigh bike was his mechanical companion, which he carried down two flights of stairs. The smell of the incinerator would linger indefinitely in the corridors of his mind with each descending step of the past. He could still recreate the anticipation of this relaxing ride to school with the ever so clear and bright light lingering in the fresh sky above. The first mile of his trip took him through a quiet and quaint neighborhood covered by the crimson rays of the sun's extending arms filled with *flamboyanes*, a native tree with deep red flowers, dripping over whitewashed fences of homes with clay tiled Spanish rooftops and stucco walls. Its flowers swayed gently in the wind. The tires of his bicycle hummed as he slowly coasted through the *calles callados* (stilled streets) adorned with multicolored petunias, hibiscus, palm trees, and red roses. The aromatic scent painted this idyllic memory as he immersed himself in it diurnally, nourishing his subconscious and conscious minds with its rejuvenating powers. His senses were stimulated by nature's indefatigable presence, an existence revered by the aborigines before the civilized world flourished. Its impact had endured and would continue to exist and reveal itself to man. How unfortunate are those who do not revel in the greatness of nature and memories.

Lance felt completely free when he rode his bicycle to school every morning possessing his own thoughts with no one there to interfere. The motion created by his bicycle, which carried him through the streets of Hato Rey and Condado, allowed him to internalize and *ensimismarse* (to search within) for his true thoughts and identity. Growing up in a foreign country, such as Puerto Rico, where people spoke a different language and had a diverse set of values, was not easy to understand or accept. Lance did not assimilate everything in the Puerto Rican culture. He learned the Spanish language, which he spoke fluently; however, he did not consider himself to be a Puerto Rican or a true North American. Although Lance did not comprehend this strife at the time, he was very taciturn and withdrawn with his thoughts, searching for his own identification with self. Little did he know at this time that he was cultivating a strong sense of independence from others and society.

Later he would embrace the aphorism by John Stuart Mill, the 19th century English writer and philosopher, who affirmed: "It is better to be an unsatisfied human than a satisfied pig. It is better to be an unsatisfied Socrates than a satisfied Socrates." The search for meaning in life, whether a person is "foraging" for his identity within a bicultural country as Lance was doing, or whether one is curious about his purpose in the world, is a quest, which all men should pursue at some time in their lives. As Mill implies, a complete understanding of life and its meaning are impossible; if such truth were easily attainable, man would search no further. Without an inquiry and pursuit for truth, man would become satisfied; therefore, his life would lose its meaning because he would no longer have to struggle to understand.

Man's quenchless thirst to discover propels him to think. Lance would never forget the endless hours he spent on the basketball court dribbling and shooting the ball. Basketball was his whole life. The concentric circles he created, pivoting to the left and right, as he dribbled and stopped to pull up for a jump shot were foundational. The unlimited dreams of running side by side with the all-time best players like Jerry West, Earl Monroe, and Walt Frasier never died. His thoughts and dreams fueled his life, actions, and reason for being. Sports and the circular image of a basketball were the fundamentals for play and deep thinking, since thoughts are constantly evolving and revolving in the mind. He strove for perfection on the court by practicing each movement and skill: mastering the dexterity of using both hands for dribbling, shooting, and passing. This discipline would transcend later as he was able to view world perspectives from divergent points of views. Most North Americans, for example, cannot navigate with ease to other countries where English is not the official language; thus, they cannot truly engage intellectually, spiritually, or socially with others. The capitalistic materialism of the United States, the most democratic country of the world, lags behind intellectually because it values technology, science, math, engineering, and medicine at the expense of foreign languages. Languages are the gateway to global communication with others and oneself.

The many lessons learned on the basketball court, such as remaining cool and calm during an intense game, were difficult to simulate in practice. The excruciating pressure, especially as an adolescent, and the constant movement were electrifying. The key was always to try to remain still and execute your movements reducing the number of mistakes. Learning how to play effectively with your teammates was just as important in a team sport. Working together with other players was satisfying and challenging, since it was easy to drift into selfish play instead of valuing the cohesiveness of the unit.

Basketball was a very gratifying and frustrating game because it was representative of life with its many highs and lows. Lance pondered this ritual of play and sports passed down through the centuries by the Greeks during the first Olympic Games. The emotion, excitement, and energy were very intense. It was a competition in which the mind, body, and spirit became one. He was reminded of the thoughts of William S. Burroughs, the author of *Naked Lunch* and precursor of the Beat Generation who influenced Jack Kerouac, another important writer of this period. These writers expressed life on a very natural and noncommittal level where man was encouraged to forget about time and routines, which enslaved him with responsibilities and false illusions created by the bourgeoisie in the 20th century. Even though these writers did not write about basketball, they wrote about man's search for meaning amongst the bums and deadbeats of society. These people lived life according to their rules and not by the ones imposed upon them by society. They lived to play and played to live much like a basketball player. A true basketball player loves his sport for the freedom and joy he experiences much like a person who lives purposefully from day to day without a worry, doing what he or she desires. But, more importantly, the Beat Generation of Burroughs and Kerouac wanted to challenge and question the status quo of society where people lived mindless and unfulfilling lives. Many were enslaved by work and material gain without any introspective stimulation for insight and meaning.

Lance would never forget the hours he spent on the basketball court as a young teenager: magical times he would cherish for the rest of his life. They taught him to take time away from work every day to ride a bicycle, run, swim, shoot some hoops, and play. He realized that a person didn't have to participate in sports to experience time away from responsibilities. This was underscored, for example, after receiving an invitation from David, a former student who became a good friend. David invited him to attend his sculpture exhibit at Santa Fe Community College in New Mexico. Lance was glad to see his buddy become a sculptor, and he wanted to be present at the exhibition if possible. They had remained friends over the years, and Lance had gotten David involved in triathlons. But, after a few years, David's interest in this sport waned. Lance encouraged him to pick up something he enjoyed, such as art. One can lose oneself in the creation of a painting or sculpture just as one can disconnect oneself from chores and work on a long bike ride or a run along the river. A life without some sort of creative endeavor and recreation for free thought is a stagnant existence.

Lance was especially concerned about American society as it entered the 21st century. Technology was overtaking our lives with the invention of the Internet where the latest news and information can be obtained instantaneously. People were spending more and more time indoors communicating with people across the world, which was good, but much of the information was not censured for children and young people. Pornography, sexual exploitation, and other immoral sites can be accessed easily by anyone. This bothered Lance because young children could be exposed to topics they were not able to understand, which could affect their moral judgment. He believed in the freedom of information, but he felt like society was advancing too quickly causing the younger generation to suffer more. Not only were computers occupying the time that one might spend walking, running, or talking with others over a cup of coffee, but people were also spending more time in front of televisions and texting from their smart phones. In addition, Americans seemed to be working more and more hours, and life just slipped by at an exceedingly fast pace.

It's important to slow down and breathe deeply. Think of life without a sunset or trees to admire. Humans are equipped with the necessary tools to experience life to its fullest, but when one ignores the spiritual effects of prayer and breathing, one deprives the soul of growth. The rhythm of the ocean surf pounding on the shore and crashing on the sand before returning to the sea is essential for man to experience. Its majestic energy communicates with the soul as he inhales and exhales. Nature is at his fingertips like the keyboard of his computer; however, he feels compelled to keep up with the news, the latest advances in medicine, and technology, which are important, as long as he maintains the equilibrium with his inner being. These distractions upset the natural clock within him that harbors all the happiness and serenity he ever needs. What else does man need? It is so simple that it eludes him because it is his deep-rooted inclination to search and decipher the unsolvable. Society teaches man to set and reach goals. Once a person accomplishes one goal, he is pressured to set another one sending him on the continuous rat race treadmill.

Jack Kerouac's novel *On the Road* was interesting, but it upset Lance to some extent. Kerouac describes the life of Dean and Sal, two bums who travel from the East Coast to the West Coast at a frenetic speed in their stolen car. On their journey they make frequent stops in Colorado, Texas, Georgia, and other states during their journey. They do a lot of drinking, and Dean bangs as many girls as possible. They hook up with other bums they have met over the years in places like New Orleans where they drink some more and listen to jazz. They talk about their carefree existence with no desire to marry, find employment, or be accountable for any type of responsibility. The only thing that is a compulsory obligation for them is to get back on the road again, moving from one place to the next. Lance enjoyed the literary style defined by its philosophy of going from one thought to the next as they rendezvoused from one coast to the other. He could really appreciate the movement, but he felt like there was something missing. Maybe, this is what Kerouac wanted to suggest in his writings. It seemed like there could be a happy medium between the bourgeoisie life of responsibility and the bum's life of irresponsibility. Kerouac foresaw the future in one respect, since our society was becoming more controlled by the advancement of technology. Society had reached a point in which man was troubled and performed as a robot marching to the beat of his superficial materialism and acquisition; nevertheless, man should not become a complete *bum* rejecting all accountability.

Lance believed people needed to become aware of their need to contribute to the well-being and preservation of peace and love among its citizens. Man should not just think of his own needs, but he should also consider those of others with regards to everything: technology, politics, education, family, and morality. He could no longer expect government to control his political decisions and redefine his freedoms, the Church to mold his religious beliefs, the school systems to dictate how to educate his children, and technology to completely sabotage his time alienating him from meditating and *walking in Nature*. Man needs to change otherwise society will self-destruct morally and spiritually.

Lance and his wife Juana had just returned to San Antonio, Texas from a two-week trip to Spain where they spent a considerable amount of time in Salamanca. As they flew over the United States, he realized the dreams of Thomas Jefferson, George Washington, Abraham Lincoln, and the other great forefathers of America were not being honored today. Everyone should go to Washington, D.C. to see the monuments and read the quotes engraved by the statues that commemorate these great figureheads because their ideals are different from the ones our society reveres today. Education was viewed as a channel to overcome ignorance and, in essence, as a way to achieve fulfillment and happiness. Today, we regard education as a means to get a good job, so one can consume and partake in the frenzy of materialism. In the 1800's man valued the spiritual aspect of education, and today he is very utilitarian worshipping the materialistic gains he can acquire. Our thirst and quest for more technology and information are examples of our superficial way of viewing the world and ourselves.

Man has become robotic ignoring the emptiness he feels within himself. The vulgar and uninhibited lyrics of his music and many of the programs he watches and accesses on his computers and televisions fuel this dissatisfaction. He denies the emotions created by a lack of moral integrity brought on by a renewed renaissance in society that destroys and alienates him from a spiritual foundation.

Medicine has advanced to such a level where people are living longer, and scientists are inventing many cures for diseases, which are essential for the longevity of mankind. Nevertheless, society wants, in a certain way, to overcome death, which is a natural component of living, and by doing this man rejects his humanness and vulnerability. The technological and medical improvements are necessary and instrumental when they aid in fostering good health and quality of life. However, they can become excessive when they prolong the life of a patient in a decadent state, keeping him alive regardless of his physical condition. In addition, technology becomes disproportionate when it takes a person away from his spirituality and connectedness with nature and other human beings. It promotes impersonal behaviors with busier work schedules; thus, it poisons one's life with more deadlines and responsibilities. Man spends less and less time with his family, friends, and himself. He doesn't connect emotionally with others because he relies almost exclusively on text messages, e-mails, faxes, and automated voice messages on smart phones. Man is advancing and moving too fast in a world that feels uncomfortable with silence, prayer, and meditation because a day full of noise and things to cross off the "to do list" have become the new norm.

Solitude for Lance was comforting because it provided the space he pursued for finding inner peace whereas many lived reacting to life through the corruptive and corrosive vacuum of thoughtlessness. The introspective drive to view the world from multiple perspectives to conclude that all men have the same inherent need to dwell within, so as to fully know oneself, was fundamental for his development. Much like the philosophers and poets of the world, Lance wanted to continue adding to his *canvas of impressions* to etch out his place in a global community with its rich diversities and complexities. This voyage began for Lance when he and his family navigated transversely across the Caribbean Sea on their way to Puerto Rico. There, against the backdrop of the rhythmic Spanish language and this new foreign frontier, he inadvertently began the process of *ensimismamiento* (turning within) to become whole as a person who continues to explore his uniqueness. This quiet place spoke to him often when he traveled. He remembered on a recent trip standing in Spain's oldest Gothic medieval cathedral in Ávila where he and his wife, Juana, experienced the vibrant presence of Santa Teresa, the mystical Spanish saint who prayed under the star-shaped cupola. Here Juana lit a candle in honor of her late mother, Joan, a godly woman with an ephemeral smile. Juana knew her mother's influence and love still resounded in her heart and in the numerous people Joan touched during her lifetime. It is this flickering flame of light that enticed Lance to sit apart and record with his pen the extraordinary moments of his brief existence. This experience brought out the *humanness* and metaphors within him to connect with others and to be completely present before its brightness extinguished leaving its imprint in the wake of the vanishing smoke.

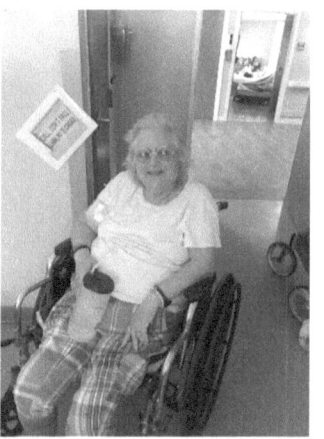

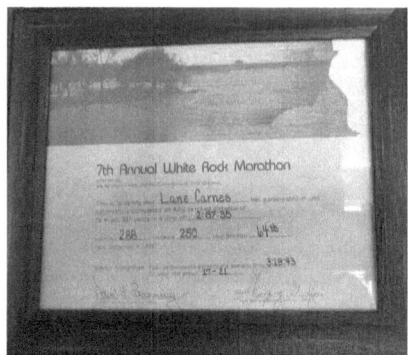

Coach Ivan Marquez, Orlando Alvarez, George Alexakos, Morey Rothenberg, Luis Davila, David Hood, Ruben Priegues, Gregg Dewalt, Rudy Betancourt, Lane Carnes, Ed Alvarez.

Sue Howe, Sue Ames, Jennifer Fibbe, Elsie Jerez, Terry O'Donnell, Sylvette Ortiz, Evelyn Ortiz.

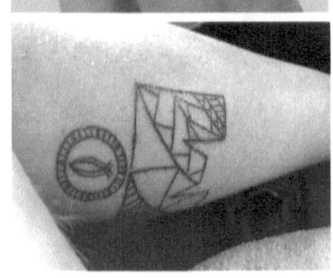

SPORTS IN BRIEF

Wesleyan Rallies To Trim Hawks

The Wesleyan Academy Eagles outshot Robinson 9-2 in the final 48 seconds and went on to register a 68-62 victory Thursday in PRHSAA basketball conference game.

The Eagles, playing on their home court, stormed back from an 11-point halftime deficit and finally grabbed the lead for good 61-60 on Vinnie Calvente's layup off a fastbreak with 48 seconds left.

Calvente, who picked up four fouls in the first half, finished with a game-high 26 points while Zeke Lopez tallied another 14. Ed Alvarez and Lane Carnes scored 15 and 12 respectively for the Hawks, who led 34-23 at halftime.

The victory boosted the Eagles into a second place tie with the Hawks in the B Division. Both teams own 5-2 records.

golf

Lane Carnes, Rick Schultz, Jim Rayson, Jim Hoover, George Barrera, Stuart Levin, Jim Reye, Chuck Irsch, Monica Stevenson, Tina McKenna, David Fisch, Debbie White, John Lehr, Philip Meilunas, Sue Howe, Amy Stripe, Sylvette Ortiz, Coach Gary Twaits.

www.ingramcontent.com/pod-product-compliance
Lightning Source LLC
LaVergne TN
LVHW091547060526
838200LV00036B/735